8

DEAD MOUNT
DEATH PLAY

STORY RYOHGO NARITA
ART SHINTA FUJIMOTO

CONTENTS

DEAD MOUNT
DEATH PLAY

#62

POLKA SHINOYAMA.

...IT SEEMS THEIR SOLE MISSION IS THE SURVEILLANCE AND PROTECTION OF THIS KID.

I ANALYZED THE PHONES OF THE PEOPLE KEEPING AN EYE ON THE BUILDING IN QUESTION, BUT...

FORTUNES... DO YOU SUPPOSE HE CAN REALLY SEE THE FUTURE?

LOOKS LIKE A GIRL FROM THE SHINOYAMA FAMILY IS ALSO STAYING IN THAT BUILDING.

BUT THE ONE THEY'RE PAYING PARTICULAR ATTENTION TO IS POLKA-KUN, THE KID WHO'S TELLING FORTUNES.

GOOD QUESTION. NOWADAYS, YOU'LL FIND SOME WHO ARE YOUTUBERS AND THE LIKE.

DO YOU THINK IT'S TYPICAL IN THIS COUNTRY FOR HIGH SCHOOLERS TO OPEN FORTUNE-TELLING SHOPS?

WHO KNOWS? THEN AGAIN, FORTUNES AREN'T ONLY ABOUT SEEING THE FUTURE.

IT'S POSSIBLE THERE'S MORE THAN ONE ORGANIZATION KEEPING TABS OVER THERE.

EITHER WAY, I FELT LIKE THE AREA AROUND THE BUILDING WAS UNDER PRETTY STRICT SURVEILLANCE, DIDN'T YOU?

FROM THE LOOKS OF IT, THE MAJORITY OF THEM ARE JUST SMALL-TIME CHUMPS...

...BUT THERE WERE SOME WHO SEEMED LIKE THEY HAD REAL POTENTIAL.

YOU'RE THE ONE WHO TOLD ME TO KEEP IT STEALTHY, REMEMBER, BOSS?

I'M IMPRESSED YOU DIDN'T MAKE A MOVE ON THEM.

YEAH. AND I'M GLAD YOU DID.

PATAN (SHUT)
ぱたん

WE'RE DONE HIDING AND JUST FEELING OUT THE SITUATION.

IF WE DON'T ACT, THERE'LL HAVE BEEN NO POINT IN US COMING ALL THE WAY OUT HERE.

#62

NEXT CUSTOMER, PLEASE COME IN!

SFX: KYORO (SEARCH) KYORO

WHAT'S THE MATTER, SOARA-SAN?

HOW CUTE! IS SHE A FORTUNE-TELLER TOO?

LOOKS LIKE HE'S PRETTY POPULAR.

IT'S SURPRIS-INGLY CROWDED HERE.

I'VE NEVER FELT ANYTHING LIKE THIS BEFORE...

...EVEN WHEN I WAS IN THAT GARBAGE HEAP OF A LAB.

...I JUST GOT CHILLS OR SOMETHING... DEEP IN MY BONES.

NOTHING... I DON'T KNOW WHY, BUT...

A-ARE YOU OKAY?

HMM...

I'M SO JEALOUS!

I JUST FEEL SOME-THING'S IN THE AIR.

YEAH. IT'S NOT LIKE I'M SICK.

I'M SURE YOU'VE PICKED UP ON SOMETHING.

?

AN UNKNOWN POWER THAT'S NOT OF THIS WORLD!

YOU MIND... TELLING US A LITTLE MORE ABOUT IT?

YEAH? THAT'S VERY INTERESTING.

!

AFTER ALL, THE FORTUNE-TELLER HERE IS THE REAL DEAL!

WHO IS THIS GUY?

WELL, DEPENDING ON HOW YOU LOOK AT IT, YOU COULD SAY THAT.

I SEE... SO WORD ABOUT HIM HAS EVEN SPREAD ABROAD...

HUH!? YOU TRAVELED ALL THE WAY TO JAPAN JUST TO COME HERE!?

WELL, THE LAST COUPLE OF DAYS HAVE BEEN PARTICULARLY CROWDED... SEEING AS HOW THE DAY BEFORE YESTERDAY, HE TOOK A DAY OFF BECAUSE THE POLICE CAME BY.

I-IS IT ALWAYS SO BUSY?

ANY DAY I HAVE TIME, WITHOUT FAIL!

YOU'VE BEEN HERE MORE THAN ONCE?

IT HAPPENED ON THIS VERY BUILDING.

IT'S HANDS! HAAANDS!! MROWWW!!

WOW! WHAT IS THAT!?

CHECK OUT THIS VIDEO.

[LIVE] Let's teach Shinjuku crows how to talk!

SHARE   SAVE   REPORT

SUBSCRIBE

Proppen
78K Subscribers

7/11/2020 Livestream
This time I'm doing a livestream while cosplaying Killer Whale-chan from the Sharkborg from Hell series!!! I was planning on teaching words to crows in Shinjuku when I caught this crazy thing on camera!!!

...SHOWED UP AT THIS BUILDING...

"PHANTOM SOLITAIRE," THE MAN RESPONSIBLE FOR THAT EPISODE WITH THE DIRIGIBLE...

THAT'S RIGHT. THIS INCIDENT IS PRECISELY WHAT BROUGHT US HERE.

WOW...

SHOULD I INTERPRET THIS AS EVIDENCE SOLITAIRE HAS ALREADY MADE CONTACT WITH "THE SORCERER FROM THE OTHER SIDE OF THE SKY" THAT HABAKI MENTIONED?

BUT I PERSONALLY THINK OTHERWISE.

THE GENERAL CONSENSUS SEEMS TO BE IT WAS ANOTHER ONE OF SOLITAIRE'S SPECTACLES, DONE JUST FOR THE FUN OF IT.

IF SO, CAN SOLITAIRE USE SORCERY...?

BUT THE SCALE OF WHAT HE DOES IS ALWAYS PROPORTIONATE TO THE NUMBER OF PEOPLE HE KNOWS ARE WATCHING.

SOLITAIRE NEVER ACTS WITH A PLAN.

HE'S SPONTANEOUS AND UNMETHODICAL.

IT DOESN'T MAKE SENSE FOR HIM TO PULL SUCH AN INCREDIBLE FEAT WITHOUT ANY FOREWARNING ON A ROOFTOP IN SHINJUKU AT NIGHT.

YOU THINK SOME MYSTERY PHENOMENON ATTACKED SOLITAIRE?

SO YOU PROPOSE THAT WASN'T JUST A TRICK...

11

MAYBE HE WASN'T ATTACKED SO MUCH AS REHEARSING SOME KIND OF ELABORATE DANCE ROUTINE?

NOT NECESSARILY.

MEANING?

A MYSTERIOUS ENTITY AND A CROOK DANCING HAND IN HAND UNDER THE NIGHT SKY!

HA-HA! THAT'S QUITE A PICTURE!

PFT!

THEY LOOK LIKE THEY'RE HAVING FUN.

THEY'RE ACTING AWFULLY CHUMMY.

RIGHT? DON'T YOU THINK SO? IT'S SO ROMANTIC!

THAT'S SO... OVERLY DRAMATIC.

OH. LOOKS LIKE MY NUMBER'S UP.

TICKET NUMBER 25, PLEASE COME IN!

PITA (FREEZE)

...CAN I ASK YOU YOUR NAME?

SEE YA.

I HOPE YOU ENJOY JAPAN AND ITS MYSTERIES.

IF YOU DO A SEARCH FOR MY NAME IN ENGLISH LETTERS, YOU'LL FIND ME ON SOCIAL MEDIA. TILL THEN!

I'M MIKOTO. MIKOTO SAIMYOUJI.

MIKOTO

YEAH, I GUESS HE AND I CLICKED.

...YOU TWO SURE HIT IT OFF.

14

WHAT IS IT?

HUH...

!

ALL RIGHT! LET'S EXAMINE!

IT SEEMS THAT GUY...

MIKOTO
@mikoto_kansatsu

I'm a forensics specialist in Tokyo! Let's examine!

125 Following **14K** Followers

MIKOTO @mikoto_kans...

...IS A MEDICAL EXAMINER.

HE'S NOT COMING IN TODAY?

I'D LIKE TO GET SAIMYOUJI-SENSEI'S OPINION.

THE JOB OF A FORENSICS SPECIALIST
- Autopsies & chemical analyses
- Determining cause of death
- Identification through fingerprints and dental records
- DNA analysis
- Blood work analysis
- Psychological an[...]
- And much more

FORENSICS IS CHRONICALLY UNDERSTAFFED.

EVEN IF HE'S A "TROUBLE-MAKERS" SPECIALIST, HE MUST STILL BE BUSY.

I TOLD YOU BEFORE.

APPARENTLY, HE'S BEEN REALLY INTO THIS MEDIUM LATELY AND COMES HERE TO SEE HIM.

WHAT A LAUGH.

BOSS

HE'S PROBABLY GOT TROUBLEMAKER CASES FROM OTHER JURISDICTIONS TO DEAL WITH TOO.

FOR BEING SO BUSY, HE'S BEEN COMING OUT HERE TO SHINJUKU AN AWFUL LOT THESE DAYS.

THAT'S RIGHT. HE SAID THE FORTUNE-TELLER IS A YOUNG KID WHO SUDDENLY SHOWED UP IN TOWN.

I SEE... AND THIS MEDIUM'S IN SHINJUKU?

HUH?

HMM... A YOUNG FORTUNE-TELLER...

GASHON

GASHON

GASHON (KASHNK)

AND THAT PEN IS... INSPECTOR... HOSOROGI?

I CAN'T BELIEVE THERE WAS NEVER ANY TRICK TO THIS.

PHEW... I'VE SEEN TWENTY-FIVE PEOPLE SO FAR TODAY...

I MUST BE ABOUT HALFWAY THROUGH.

Heh-heh-heh. Looking forward to working with you, kid.

WHAT DO YOU MEAN... "OWES SO MUCH TO"?

HUH?

?

?

HMMM... I DOUBT PHANTOM SOLITAIRE HAS EVEN CONSIDERED THAT THE GUY HE OWES SO MUCH TO IS A WRITING UTENSIL.

IS THAT SO?

I'LL REPAY MY DEBT TO HOSOROGI ANOTHER TIME!

WELL, I JUST MEAN THE NIGHT FROM THAT *VIRAL VIDEO*. WHEN I FOUGHT HIM, HE SAID SOMETHING ABOUT "OWING HOSOROGI," REMEMBER?

*SOLITAIRE SPREADS LIES

...MEANT SOMETHING MUST HAVE HAPPENED TO HOSOROGI... I WAS WORRIED ABOUT HIM.

KNEW THAT A SNIPER ATTACKING ME...

SO I CAME TO SEE WHAT IT WAS ABOUT.

WARNING: XIAOYU DOESN'T KNOW IT WAS A LIE.

UNFOUNDED WORRY

COULD IT BE THAT YOUR MEMORY WAS TAMPERED WITH WHEN YOU WERE ALIVE...?

PHANTOM SOLITAIRE... WHAT ON EARTH COULD HIS OBJECTIVE BE...?

What the heck!? I'm scared! Help!

No, no, no! I have zero recollection of that guy!

*THE PEN IS BEING PLAYED

OH... YES, PLEASE.

IS IT ALL RIGHT IF I CALL IN THE NEXT PERSON?

AND THEY LEFT THE FIELDS ABOUT THEIR AGE AND GENDER BLANK FOR US.

GOING BY THEIR SURVEY, THEY'RE A TOURIST FROM ABROAD.

THEY MIGHT JUST BE DOING THIS FOR LAUGHS.

Uhhh... Sorry. I don't have much information on the next person.

THEN I'LL GET BACK TO WORK DOING CHORES.

OKAY.

POTE
(PLOP)
ぽて

IF WORSE COMES TO WORST, I'LL USE SORCERY TO PSYCHO-LOGICALLY MANIPULA—

I'LL JUST USE A SMALL SPIRIT TO SEARCH THEIR BELONGINGS AND GATHER INFORMATION.

ZU
(ZLLIP)
ズ

ZU
(ZLLIP)
ズ

THEY WON'T BE THE FIRST CLIENT WE'VE HAD LIKE THAT.

GOT IT. THANKS.

ZOKU.
(SHUDDER)

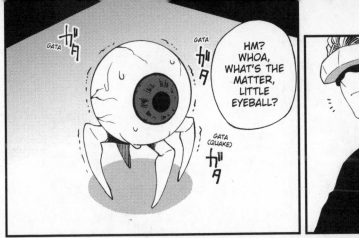

GATA

GATA

HM? WHOA, WHAT'S THE MATTER, LITTLE EYEBALL?

GATA (QUAKE)

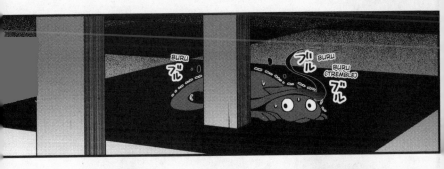

BURU

BURU

BURU (TREMBLE)

OKAY, YOU TWO WAIT HERE.

RIGHT THIS WAY!

WHAT'S THIS...? WHAT'S... COMING?

DON'T WORRY, LULU.

YOU WON'T FIND MANY WHO CAN GET THE BETTER OF THIS GUY.

A-ARE YOU GOING TO BE OKAY ON YOUR OWN?

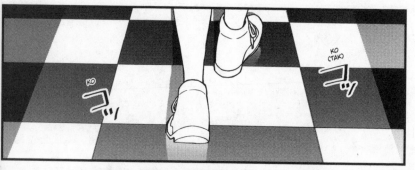

KO (TAK)

KO

IS THAT A BOY OR A GIRL?

PARDON ME.

GATA (CLATTER)

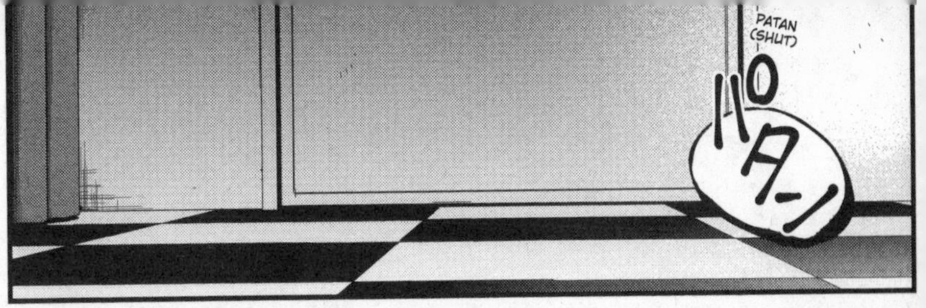
パタン
PATAN (SHUT)
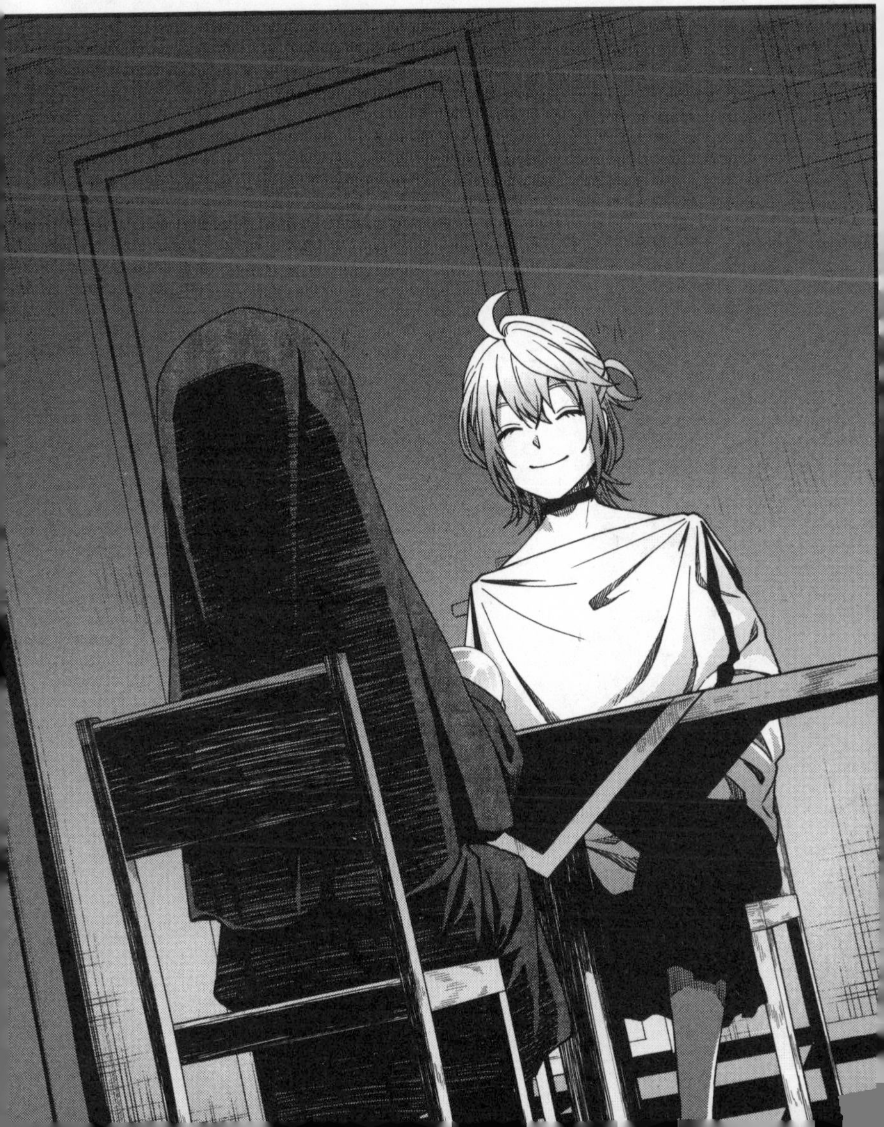

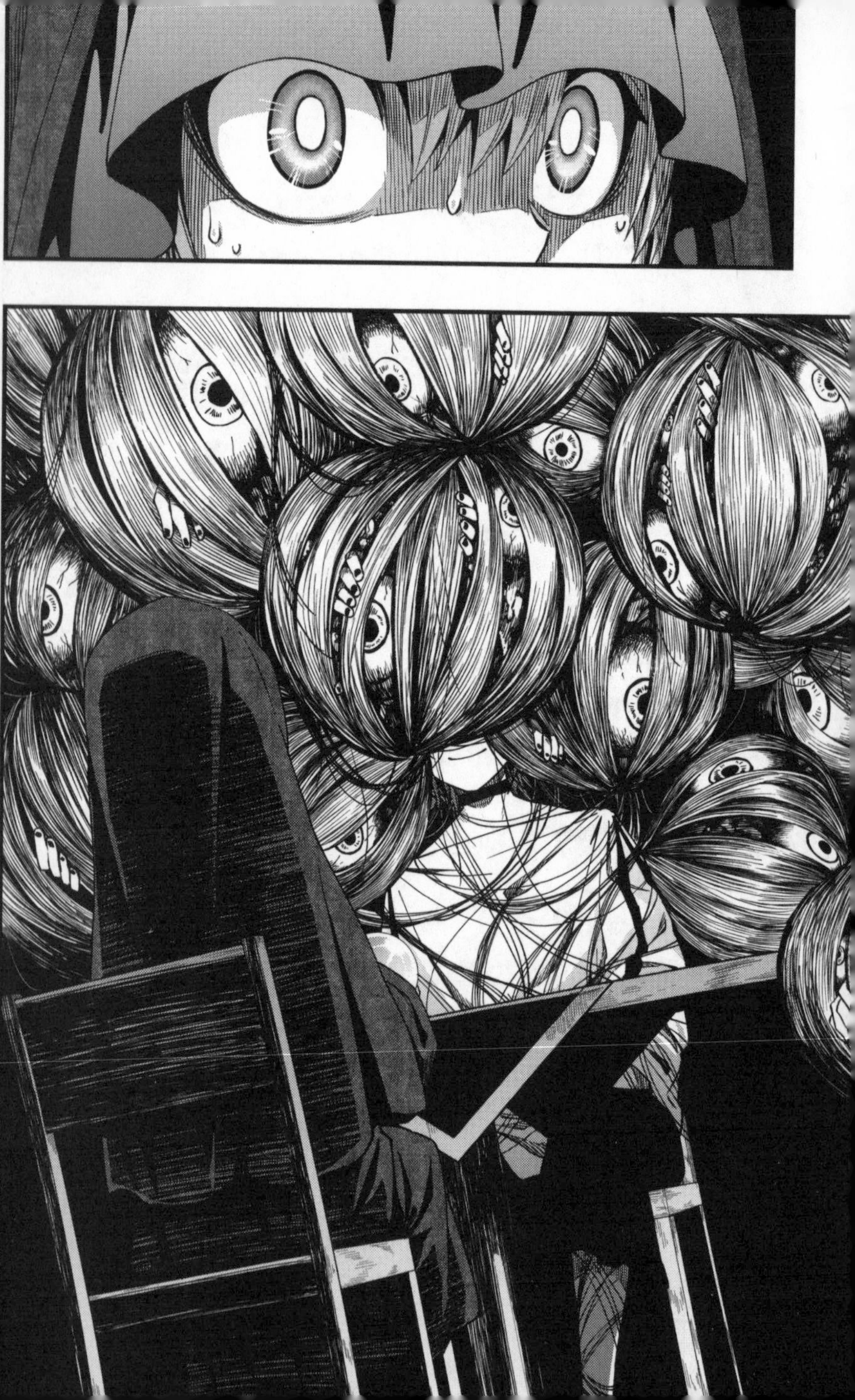

JUST... HOW MANY SOULS......? AND OVER HOW MANY YEARS......?

THIS TANGLE OF DEAD SPIRITS...

THE SPIRITS OF THE DEAD ARE GETTING IN THE WAY... I CAN'T MAKE OUT THE FACE OF THIS PERSON'S SOUL.

NOT GOOD.

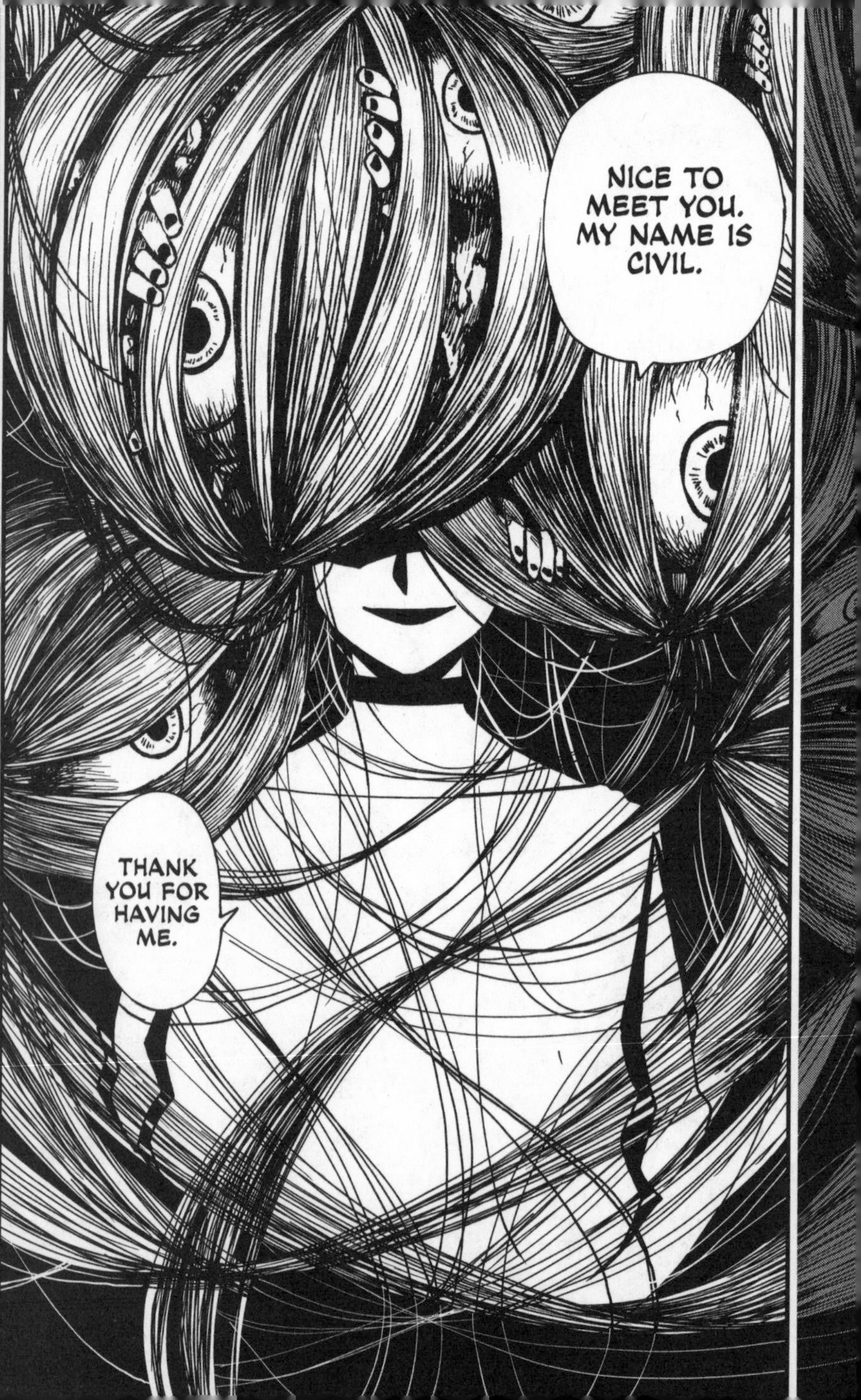
NICE TO MEET YOU. MY NAME IS CIVIL.
THANK YOU FOR HAVING ME.

#63

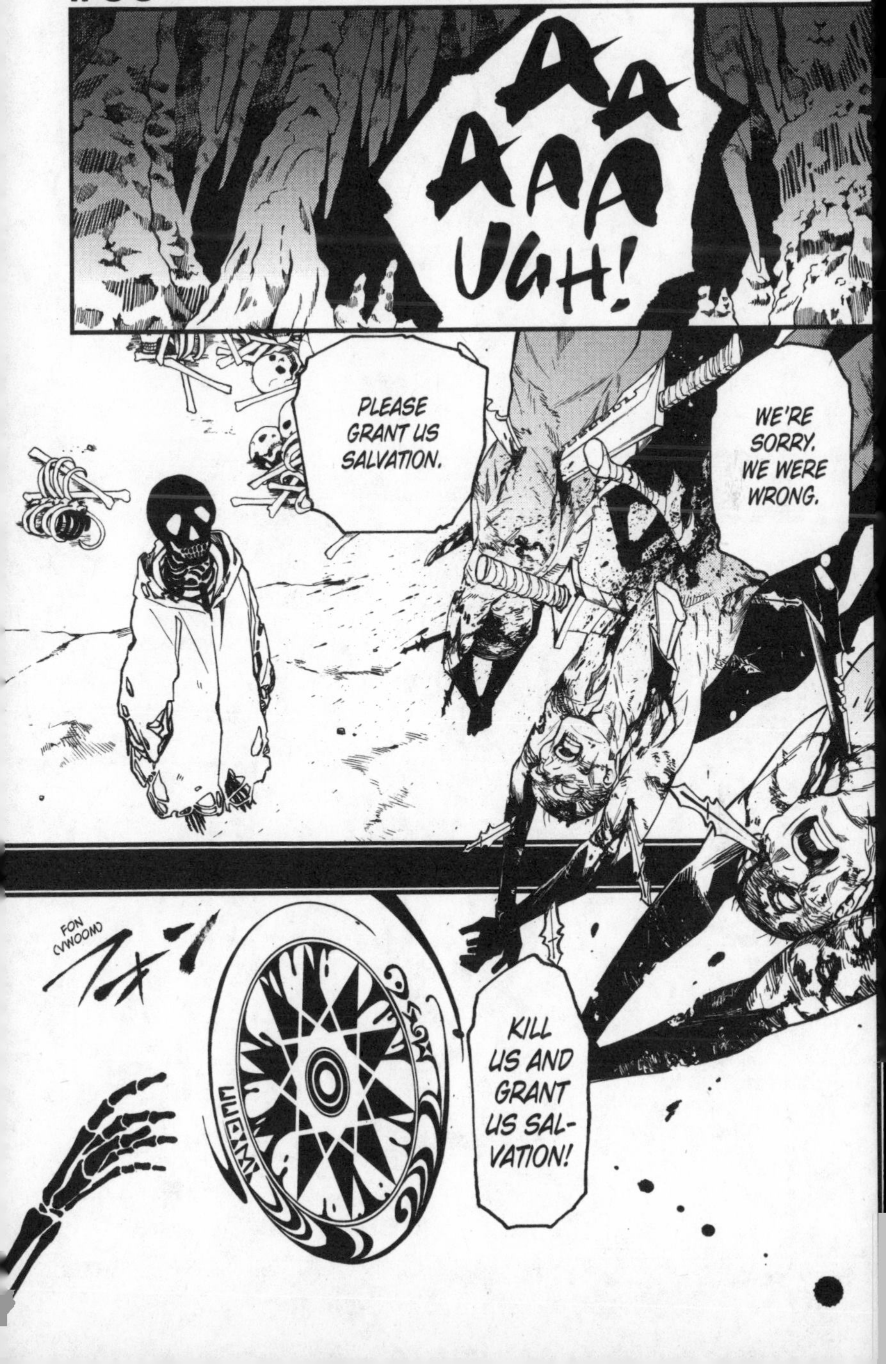
AAAAAUGH!
WE'RE SORRY. WE WERE WRONG.
PLEASE GRANT US SALVATION.
KILL US AND GRANT US SALVATION!
FON (VWOOM)

THE FIRST THING CORPSE GOD WAS REMINDED OF...

...IN HIS PREVIOUS LIFE.

...WAS THE REVENGE HE'D CARRIED OUT OVER A HUNDRED YEARS...

GAH!

EEE!

ZU (ZSH)

PETA (PAT)

PETA

AND WHAT AMASSED, AS THOUGH DRAWN TOWARD THE HORRORS.

UWAA!

AN ABANDONED MINE SHAFT OF THE DEAD, TEEMING WITH GHOSTS.

#63

TO THINK THAT IT'S NOT A PLACE BUT A SINGLE HUMAN... WHO HAS THIS MANY...

I CAN'T BELIEVE IT.

AND I'VE NEVER SEEN SPIRITS OF THE DEAD SO STRONGLY FUSED TOGETHER BEFORE.

IS SOME-THING THE MATTER?

SPIRIT EXORCISM

ZUZOZO (SUCK)

ZOZO

NO NEED TO BE FORMAL. YOU CAN CALL ME BIG BROTHER SHULA, 'KAY? WHAT DO YOU SAY?

UTSUROJUZA
REAL NAME: SHULA ZOOZOLOZO
CRAMPLAMP LAMPTON

...IF IT WERE JUST A MATTER OF QUANTITY, SHULA WOULD RETURN FROM BATTLEFIELDS WITH A SIMILAR NUMBER CLINGING TO HIM, BUT...

THE MASTER WOULD TAKE CARE OF THEM IN AN INSTANT WHEN THAT HAPPENED...

THESE PARTICULAR SPIRITS OF THE DEAD HAVE BEEN "MATURING" FOR DECADES AND DECADES.

EVEN IF THIS PERSON HAD JUST COME BACK FROM SLAUGHTERING MILLIONS ON A BATTLEFIELD, IT WOULDN'T BE LIKE THIS.

BUT THIS IS DIFFERENT.

ONLY A VERY FEW OF THESE SPIRITS BEAR ILL WILL AGAINST THIS PERSON...

IF THEY WERE LIKE THE VICTIMS OF LEMMINGS THAT CLUNG ON TO HIM...

...I COULD UNDERSTAND THEM FEARING HIS STRENGTH AND THEIR COMPETING FEELINGS OF FEAR AND LOATHING.

...IS IT OBSESSION...?

THE MAJORITY FEEL NEITHER REGRET NOR LOVE BUT RATHER...

I'LL CAST THE SPELL OF "FALSE FACE" ON MYSELF...

...AND PASTE ON A "SERENE SMILE."

I'D BETTER NOT LET MY ANXIETY SHOW.

SU (SWF)

I DON'T KNOW WHAT'S GOING ON, BUT...THIS PERSON IS DANGEROUS.

...OH?

IT APPEARS TO ME... YOU'VE BEEN ABLE TO LEAD A FULL LIFE SO FAR.

IF YOU CORRECTLY CONFRONT THOSE ENCOUNTERS, IT WILL LIKELY QUENCH YOUR SOUL'S THIRST.

YOU SAID YOU WANT TO KNOW ABOUT NEW ENCOUNTERS ...

EVERYONE AROUND ME SAYS I'VE GOT IT GOOD, BUT IT'S BEEN SURPRISINGLY DULL.

THAT'S PROBABLY BECAUSE YOU'VE BEEN DESENSITIZED TO YOUR CIRCUM- STANCES.

THAT'S A VAGUE ANSWER THAT CAN BE TAKEN ANY WHICH WAY.

HMM...

I CAN'T MAKE UP MY MIND WHETHER HE'S A FRAUD OR THE REAL THING...

APPAR-
ENTLY
SO.

THAT REMINDS ME. THAT AMAZING CRIMINAL SOLITAIRE CAME TO THIS BUILDING, DIDN'T HE?

...EN-
COUN-
TERS...

LET'S PRY A LITTLE, THEN.

NO.

SO YOU HAVEN'T MET HIM.

THOUGH IT IS POSSIBLE THAT I JUST HAVEN'T NOTICED...

I'D LOVE TO GAZE INTO HIS FUTURE TOO.

I HEAR HE'S VERY PASSIONATE ABOUT MYSTERIES.

...AND OUR FATES HAVE ALREADY CROSSED.

...AND ALL OF TODAY MESSING AROUND ON THE COMPUTER... WHAT ARE YOU TRYING TO DO?

...YOU SPENT ALL DAY YESTERDAY TAKING PHOTOS...

I KNEW IT. THIS COMPUTER'S FUNCTIONS ARE SEVERELY LACKING. I SHOULD'VE ASKED NANNY TO PUT THIS TOGETHER.

HMM...

SEE YA.

⁉

I'M HUNGRY, SO I'M HEADING HOME.

BUT AT LEAST I NEVER ONCE CONSIDERED ABANDONING THE PROJECT AND RETURNING HOME FOR A SPELL, RIGHT?

IT'S JUST A LITTLE MISCHIEF.

COME NOW.

LOOK, MORE IMPORTANTLY... DID YOU CUT OFF THE CELL PHONE YOU TOOK OFF ME?

IT'S OKAY. I BELIEVE IN YOU!

PLEASE DON'T ASK FOR THE IMPOSSIBLE.

NOW, GIVE ME A COOLER, MORE CELEBRITY-WORTHY SMILE.

YOU NEEDN'T WORRY ABOUT THAT.

THE POLICE MIGHT TRACK DOWN THE SIGNAL AND COME HERE...

DEPENDING ON HOW THINGS GO DOWN, THEY CAN PUT ME THROUGH A HELL WORSE THAN DEATH.

YOU FEAR THE POLICE MORE THAN YOU DO ME?

...THAT CELL PHONE WAS EXPENSIVE...

WE HAVE ALREADY BURNED IT.

BON CRWSHIO

36

WHAT'S THAT MEAN? I WAS JUST REMEMBERING THIS SCARY POLICE OFFICER NAMED ARASE.

SABARA-MOND...?

EVEN COMPARED TO THE BASTARD CHILDREN OF SABARA-MOND?

THEN YOU AND I ARE COMRADES!

PACHIN (SNAP)

ぱちん

HUH?

NO, I HAVE NO IDEA WHAT YOU'RE TALKING ABOUT.

SO YOU'RE NOT FAMILIAR WITH THEM EITHER?

HMM...

HOW ABOUT WE DIG IT OUT?

THE SECRET BEHIND THIS "SABARAMOND" OR WHATEVER IT IS...

BY JOINING FORCES.

Nanny

Time stamp:
Recipient:

I've completed it, so give it a look-see, sonny. The commission fee can go into the usual bank account. Now be sure to eat properly and stay warm.

PhantomSolitairesHeartracingPrankOperation.zip

◢ Today
✉ Dangerous

✉ Nanny

THEN I'VE GOT A BAD FEELING ABOUT GIVING THIS PERSON THE REINS IN THIS CONVERSATION... TIME TO CHANGE THE SUBJECT.

THE FACT THAT HE'S RAISED THE SUBJECT OF SOLITAIRE... MEANS HE'S... TRYING TO FIND OUT SOMETHING ABOUT OUR SITUATION HERE...?

...AH, YES. WELL, FOR EXAMPLE...

CAN I ASK YOU A LITTLE MORE ABOUT THAT?

...I UNDERSTAND YOU WANT TO KNOW ABOUT A "FATE THAT SPANS A HUNDRED YEARS" IN THE FLOW OF DESTINY...IS THAT RIGHT?

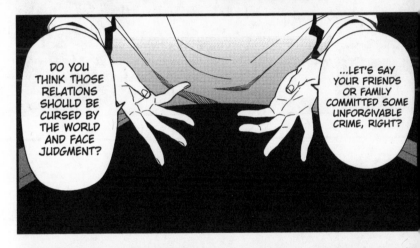

DO YOU THINK THOSE RELATIONS SHOULD BE CURSED BY THE WORLD AND FACE JUDGMENT?

...LET'S SAY YOUR FRIENDS OR FAMILY COMMITTED SOME UNFORGIVABLE CRIME, RIGHT?

CORRUPTED.

DON'T LET THEIR SPIRITS FALL TO THE NECROMANCER.

THEY'RE CORRUPTED.

COR-RUPTED.

GRANT SALVATION TO THE CORRUPTED CHILDREN.

...THIS IS JUST MY PERSONAL FEELING, BUT...

I SEE.

WELL, USUALLY THAT'S THE CASE.

...I'D LIKE TO THINK THIS WORLD ISN'T LIKE THAT.

DOES THIS SWARM OF DEAD SPIRITS HAVE SOMETHING TO DO WITH THAT...?

BUT NOT ALWAYS. MY FRIENDS AND I ARE THE TARGET OF SOME TROUBLESOME CHARACTERS.

THEIR HATRED, INCURRED A HUNDRED YEARS AGO, PERSISTS TO THIS DAY, AND WE'VE BEEN EXILED FOR IT.

OR...AN INNOCENT PERSON WHO'S BEING WRONGLY PERSECUTED?

THE GRANDCHILD OF A RUTHLESS KILLER?

THE CHILD OF A DICTATOR?

"TERRI-BLE"... YOU SAY.

IT'S THE OTHER WAY AROUND, MR. FORTUNE-TELLER.

IF THERE'S ANYTHING I CAN DO, ALLOW ME TO OFFER WHATEVER HELP I AM ABLE.

...THAT'S TERRIBLE.

MY DIVINATIONS SERVE TO FIND THE GUIDEPOSTS THAT WILL ENABLE YOU TO AVOID SUCH UNREASONABLE SITUATIONS.

THINK ABOUT IT.

...HUH?

I *WANT* TO ENCOUNTER THOSE UNREASONABLE SITUATIONS AS SOON AS POSSIBLE.

THE MORE UNREASON-ABLE, THE BETTER.

THE REASON WE'RE KICKED DOWN, THE REASON WE'RE DESPISED, THE REASON WE'RE HATED, OR THE REASON WHY WE'VE EARNED THEIR MALICE...

SAY THERE'S A CONFLICT THAT WILL LEAVE YOU TAKING THE BLAME. EVEN IF YOU COME OUT ON TOP, YOU WOULDN'T FEEL VERY GOOD, RIGHT?

...WHAT DO YOU...

...MEAN EXACTLY?

BUT IF THIS CONFLICT INVOLVES SOMEONE WHO'S HOLDING THIS RIDICULOUS HATE AGAINST YOU, THEN YOU DON'T HAVE TO WORRY ABOUT THAT.

YOU CAN FALSELY ACCUSE YOUR ADVERSARY, PUBLICLY HUMILIATE THEM, OR EVEN GRIND THEIR FLESH TO PULP, AND IT'S ALL OKAY.

TSUUU (SWFFF)

WHEN YOU HIT BACK, SMASH THEM DOWN, AND KILL THEM IN TURN, YOU ACCRUE NO LOSSES.

YOU CAN RETURN UNREASONABLE ACTION WITH UNREASONABLE ACTION.

YOU CAN CRUSH INSECTS WITH A CLEAR CONSCIENCE.

ISN'T THAT... DOING THE SAME THING AS YOUR ADVERSARY?

EVEN IF I WERE TO MAIM THEIR FAMILY RIGHT IN FRONT OF THEM, I WOULD FEEL NO REMORSE OVER IT.

YEP. THAT'S WHY THIS IS A PROBLEM OF ORDER OF OPERATIONS.

OF COURSE, WE'LL LEAVE THE MATTER OF "JUSTICE" OUT OF THE EQUATION FOR NOW, OKAY?

MY RELATIVE COMMITTED THE WRONG-DOING FIRST.

IF MY ADVERSARY SOUGHT REVENGE AGAINST JUST THAT RELATIVE, THEY WOULD HAVE EVERY RIGHT TO DO SO.

CRIME

REVENGE

...THAT STARTS A WHOLE NEW ATTACK.

CRIME

REVENGE

BUT IF THE ADVERSARY HATES *ME* FOR THE SOLE REASON THAT I AM RELATED TO THE WRONG-DOER...

IF SO...

...BE ALLOWED TO MAKE A MOVE AGAINST MY ADVERSARY'S RELATIVE?

...SHOULD I NOT IN TURN...

AFTER ALL, IT WAS MY ADVERSARY WHO ACTED UNREASONABLY FIRST.

PACHI
PACHI (CLAP)
PACHI
PACHI
PACHI
PACHI!
PACHI!

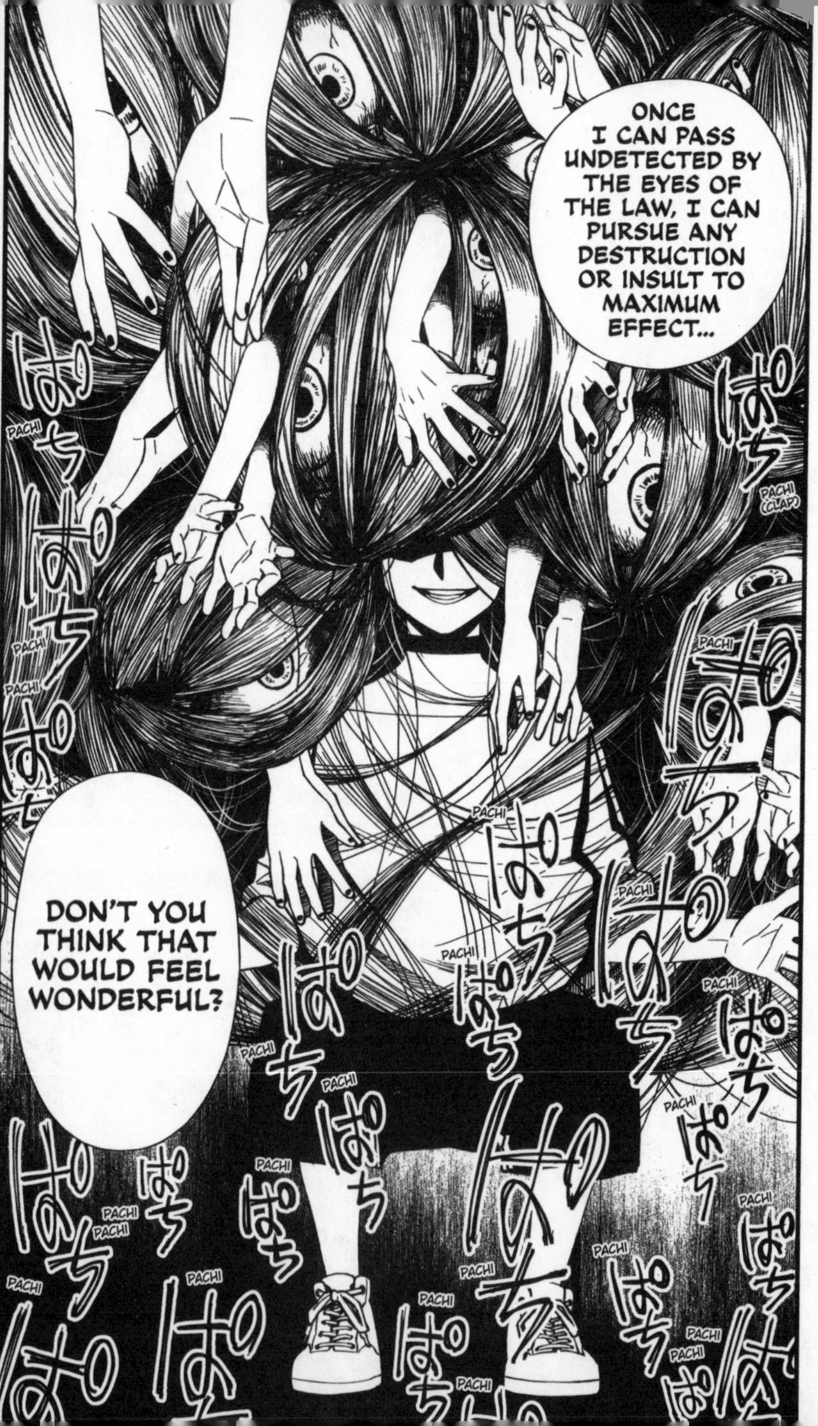
ONCE I CAN PASS UNDETECTED BY THE EYES OF THE LAW, I CAN PURSUE ANY DESTRUCTION OR INSULT TO MAXIMUM EFFECT...
ぱち
PACHI (CLAP)
DON'T YOU THINK THAT WOULD FEEL WONDERFUL?
ぱちぱち
PACHI PACHI

THIS PERSON...

...IS NOT ON THE SAME SIDE OF THINGS AS THOSE CHILDREN.

BACK WHEN I WAS "CORPSE GOD"...

...JUST BEING WITH ME...

...GOT THOSE CHILDREN KILLED FOR NO REASON. HE'S NOT LIKE THEM.

GU (CLENCH)

HE'S MORE AKIN TO...

THOSE VILLAINS BURNED EVERYONE ALIVE WITHOUT FEAR OF RETRIBUTION.

...THE SOLDIERS FROM THE GELDWOOD CHURCH, AGAINST WHOM I SOUGHT REVENGE.

IT'S JUST...FOR A SADISTIC PERVERT... THERE'S AN UNSETTLING INTENSITY ABOUT HIM...

WHO IS THIS PERSON? HE SURE SAYS...A LOT OF DISTURBING THINGS...

......

DO YOU MEAN EVERYTHING YOU JUST SAID?

ALLOW ME TO ASK YOU ONE THING...

ALL RIGHT... I UNDERSTAND WHERE YOU'RE COMING FROM.

...SOMETHING THE MATTER?

MAYBE YOU SHOULD TRY DIVINING IT TO SEE?

...WHAT DO YOU THINK?

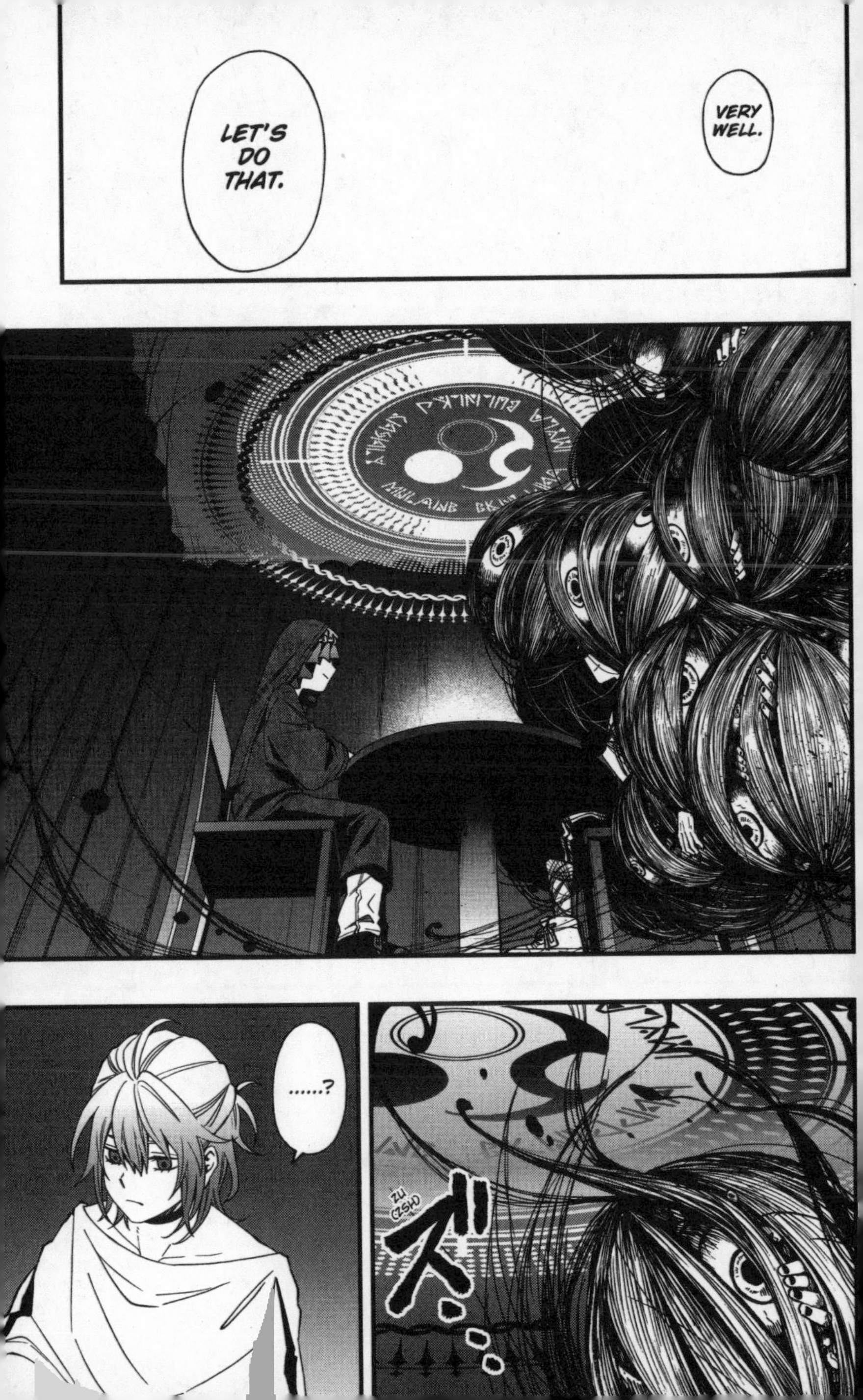
VERY WELL.
LET'S DO THAT.
ZU (ZSH)
......?

......?

ZOKU
(CHILL)

OKAY,
NOW IF
YOU'D
PLEASE
FILL OUT
THIS
SURVEY...

POLKA-
KUN?

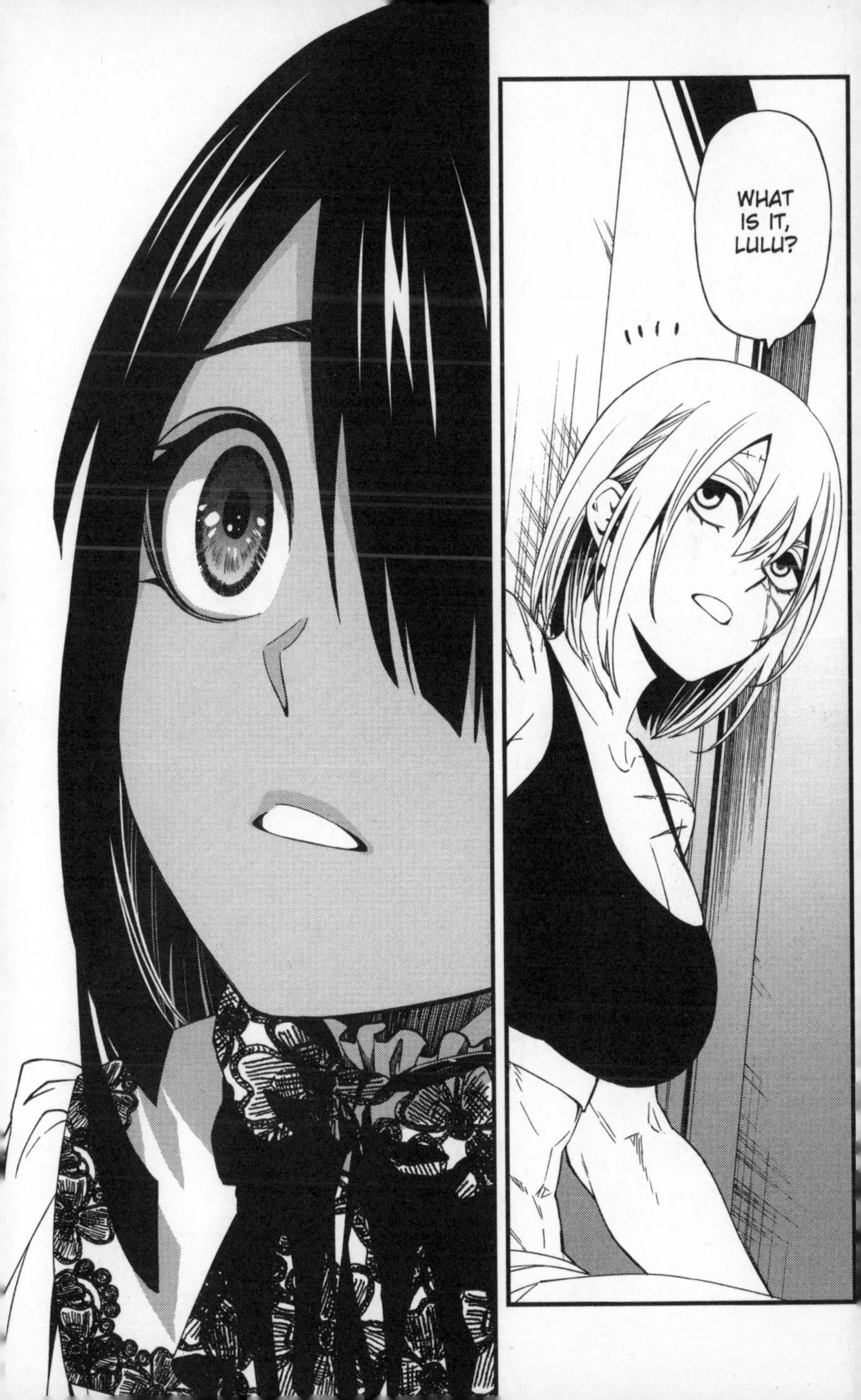
WHAT IS IT, LULU?

THEY LET ME USE THE BATHROOM.

SEE YOU TOMORROW!

COULD IT BE...

SLI (FWIP)

...EVERYONE BUT ME GETS TO GO HOME...?

ENTER THE NEXT DAY

#64

......

THE MOOD'S SHIFTED ...

... WHAT'S THIS?

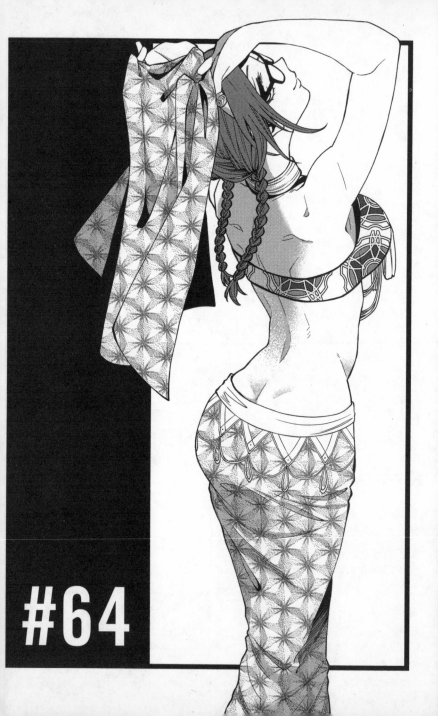

#64

HUH...? I DON'T FEEL SO GOOD...

FOR SOME REASON... I HAVE TO GET HOME...

I FEEL LIKE...I'M FORGETTING SOME- THING...

I-I'M SORRY, I'M GOING TO HAVE TO CANCEL FOR TODAY...

WHAT'S GOING ON!?

ど゛る
DORO

ど゛る
DORO
(PLOD)

UM...?

HUH?

...... WHAT IS IT, LULU?

......? SOME-THING'S GIVING ME THE CREEPS...

ZOKU (CHILL)

......!

...I CAN HEAR IT.

NO, IT'S DIFFERENT.

IS THIS... MY SENSE OF KNOWING?

THAT NUMBER... HASN'T CHANGED.

I SENSE ONE ELEMENTAL.

AT THE VERY LEAST, IT MEANS HE'S NOT LIKE ME. HE DOESN'T POSSESS THE EVIL EYE, WHICH WOULD HAVE ALLOWED HIM TO SEE THE DEAD AND GHOSTS.

HE HASN'T FIGURED OUT WHAT I'M DOING.

IN THAT CASE, I'LL GIVE HIS SENSES A SHAKE AND TOUCH HIS SOUL DIRECTLY.

CALM YOUR HEART...AND ENTRUST IT TO THE FLUCTUATIONS OF THIS SPACE.

QUITE THE OPPOSITE... THEY'RE TRYING TO PROTECT ME...?

THESE SPIRITS... THEY AREN'T AFRAID OF ME...

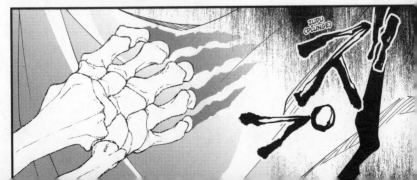

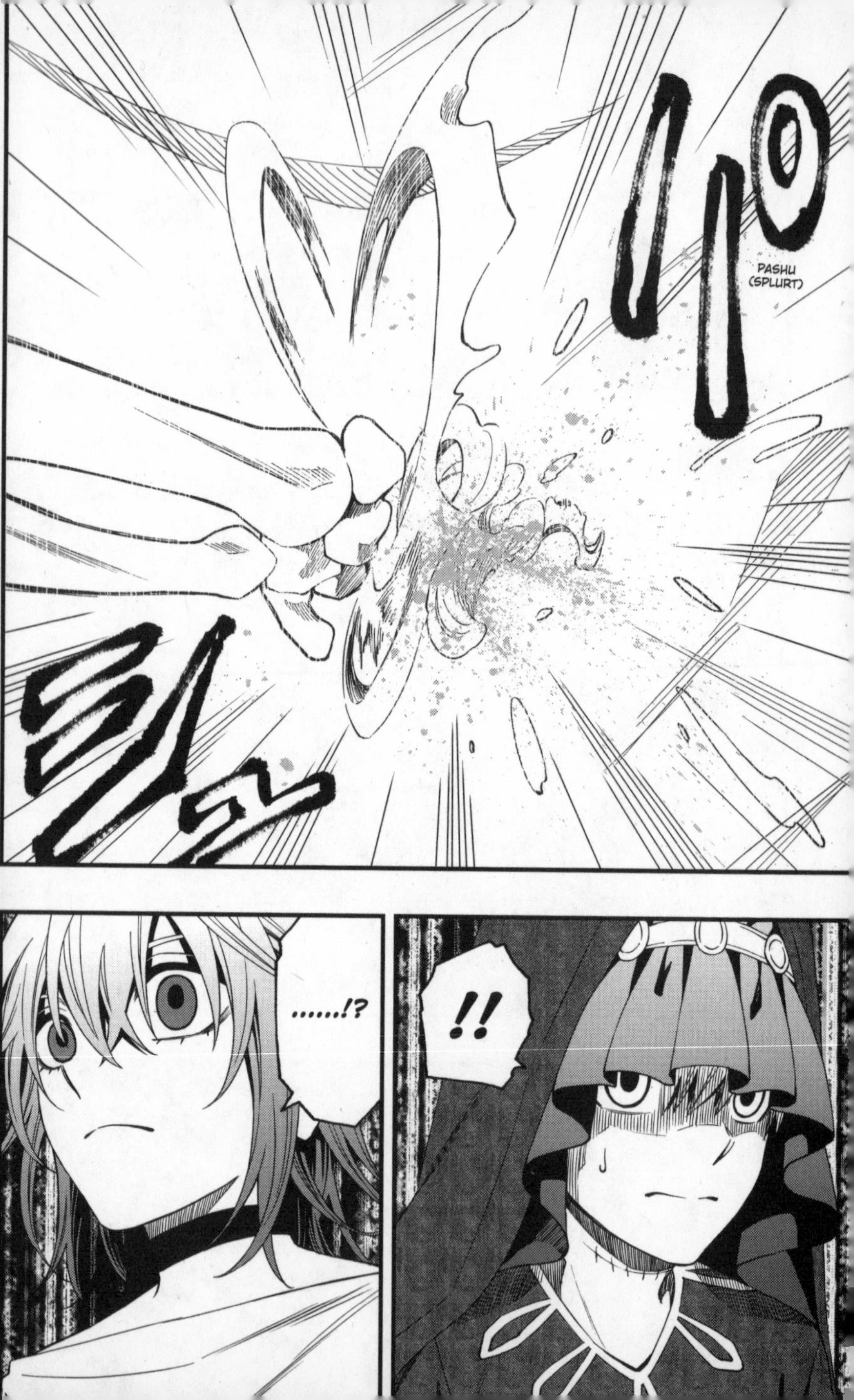
PASHU
(SPLURT)
......!?
!!

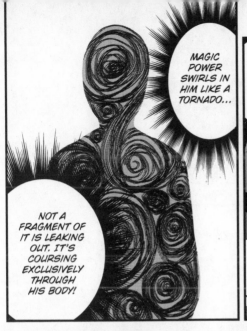

MAGIC POWER SWIRLS IN HIM LIKE A TORNADO...

NOT A FRAGMENT OF IT IS LEAKING OUT. IT'S COURSING EXCLUSIVELY THROUGH HIS BODY!

WHAT... IS THIS!?

IS HE... REALLY EVEN A HUMAN OF THIS WORLD!?

SUCH DENSE MAGIC POWER... IS ON PAR WITH THE IMPERIAL COURT SORCERERS!

THE MAGIC IN MY BODY JUST BURST.

WHAT WAS THAT?

I COULDN'T DO ANYTHING...! ANYTHING AT ALL...!!

I MESSED UP...!

DID I LEAVE ANY TRACES OF MY MEDDLING!?

DID SOMETHING JUST ATTEMPT TO INTERFERE WITH IT?

WHAT JUST HAPPENED TO ME?

JUST AS I FIGURED.

THIS IS A SENSATION I'VE NEVER EXPERIENCED BEFORE.

THIS BOY... IS A VISITOR FROM ANOTHER WORLD...?

THAT VIDEO...

...AND THIS FEELING.

NO DOUBT ABOUT IT.

SO IS HE A DECOY? A STAND-IN? A KIND OF ILLUSION?

THE THING IS... I'VE DONE MY RESEARCH ON POLKA SHINOYAMA'S BIRTH...

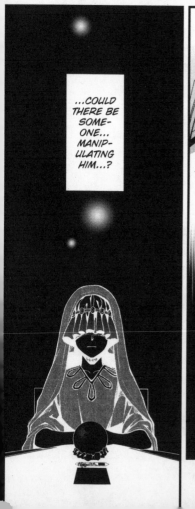

...COULD THERE BE SOME-ONE... MANIP-ULATING HIM...?

OR MAYBE...

PERHAPS HE'S THE DESCENDANT OF A STOWAWAY?

INTER-ESTING.

!

JUST NOW...DID YOU DO SOMETHING TO ME?

...WHAT AN ODD FEELING.

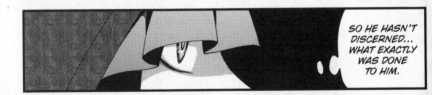

SO HE HASN'T DISCERNED... WHAT EXACTLY WAS DONE TO HIM.

IN THIS CASE, I SHOULD BE ABLE TO TAKE OVER THE SPIRITS OF THE DEAD AND KEEP AN EYE ON HIM.

STAY COOL.

I'LL LET HIM GO WITHOUT A FUSS SO HE DOESN'T GROW SUSPICIOUS OF US.

FOR THE REPLENISHING OF HIS MAGIC POWER...

...UPROOTING THESE SPIRITS OF THE DEAD AND **STEALING** THEM WOULD CERTAINLY BE A CHANGE HE'D PICK UP ON.

IT COULD HAVE BEEN THE DORMANT FATE WITHIN YOU AWAKENING...

WELL THEN... WHAT DID YOU FEEL?

AT LEAST...

HMM...

I CAN'T WAIT TO SEE WHAT COMES OUT OF IT.

PLEASE ALLOW ME... TO SEARCH YOUR SOUL A LITTLE DEEPER.

...WHAT'S LURKING INSIDE ME......

I TOO AM EAGER TO KNOW...

...ABOUT YOUR TRUE SELF...

...YOU MIGHT BE HAPPIER NOT KNOWING...

!

OOPS, SORRY. THEY'RE WITH ME.

CIVIL-SAMA!

IT TOLD ME THAT... IT'S *UNDER SOME KIND OF ATTACK...!*

I RECEIVED A *GUID-ANCE!*

THIS PLACE... IS DAN-GEROUS!

WHAT IS IT?

68

QUIT IT, BOSS.

LULU'S EARS ARE NEVER WRONG.

THE BUG'S PEOPLE MIGHT BE SETTING FIRE TO THIS PLACE.

...WE WERE JUST GETTING TO THE GOOD PART. ARE YOU SURE YOU CAN'T TAKE CARE OF IT FOR ME?

!

IS SHE REFERRING TO "FIRE-BREATHING BUG"? WAIT...MORE IMPORTANTLY...

BUG... DID SHE JUST SAY "BUG"?

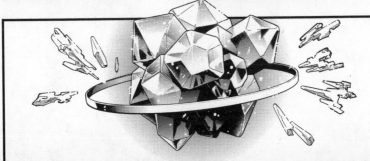

A STONE ELEMENTAL...

AND IT'S OF A RELATIVELY HIGH RANK...!

IS SHE AN ELEMENTALIST!?

WHO IS THIS YOUNG GIRL!?

NOT THE GIRL, BUT... THE... ELEMENTAL?

I REMEMBER... SEEING THIS BEFORE...

NO... HOLD ON.

SO THAT'S WHAT HAPPENED TO THIS CHILD. TO BE SOLD WHILE STILL SO YOUNG...

...BUT APPARENTLY, THE EVIL EYE WAS TOO MUCH FOR THEM.

HIS FAMILY SHOULD NATURALLY BE ABLE TO SEE ELEMENTALS...

... HONORABLE CHANCELLOR?

YOU'RE ONLY ABLE TO HEAR THE VOICES OF ELEMENTALS, ARE YOU NOT...

BYANDY EMPIRE CHANCELLOR LEUF VELLIZE

IT MUST BE MUCH HARDER FOR YOU THAN IT IS FOR US, WHO HAVE ONLY ONE OR THE OTHER.

HMM......THE EVIL EYE IS SIMULTANEOUSLY BOTH THE EYES AND THE EARS.

FOR ELEMENTALS AND SPIRITS OF THE DEAD ALIKE ARE CONSTANT COMPANIONS AT OUR SIDE.

BUT YOU SHOULD LIVE ON IN STRENGTH.

...THAT THOU SUPPORT THIS EMPIRE AS A SUBORDINATE OF HIS ROYAL EMPEROR AND AS OUR COLLEAGUE.

I WILL SIMPLY PRAY TO THE ELEMENTALS AND ASK OF THOU...

...SO THAT'S IT...

THE COLOR OF HER SOUL IS...

AND... THIS OTHER WOMAN AS WELL...

BUT THERE ARE **THREE** OF THEM. THREE PEOPLE DEEPLY CLAD IN THE COLORS OF MY FORMER WORLD.

THEN THIS WAS INEVITABLE.

IF IT WERE JUST ONE, I'D BE ABLE TO CALL IT A COINCIDENCE.

THESE THREE WHO HAVE COME TO SEE ME...

...ARE VISITORS FROM THE OTHER WORLD —!!

I'LL COME SEE YOU AGAIN. NEXT TIME...IT'LL BE AS A FRIEND.

...SORRY, MR. FORTUNE-TELLER.

NO, I MUSTN'T STIR UP TROUBLE NOW.

...I PRAY THAT THE PATH YOU WALK IS THE RIGHT ONE.

WHAT DO I DO...? SHOULD I STOP THEM ......?

KURU
(TURN)

C'MON, LET'S SPLIT.

EVEN THOUGH I HAD MY SPIRITS OF THE DEAD LEAD OUT ALL THE PEOPLE WAITING, THERE ARE STILL EYES WATCHING THIS BUILDING.

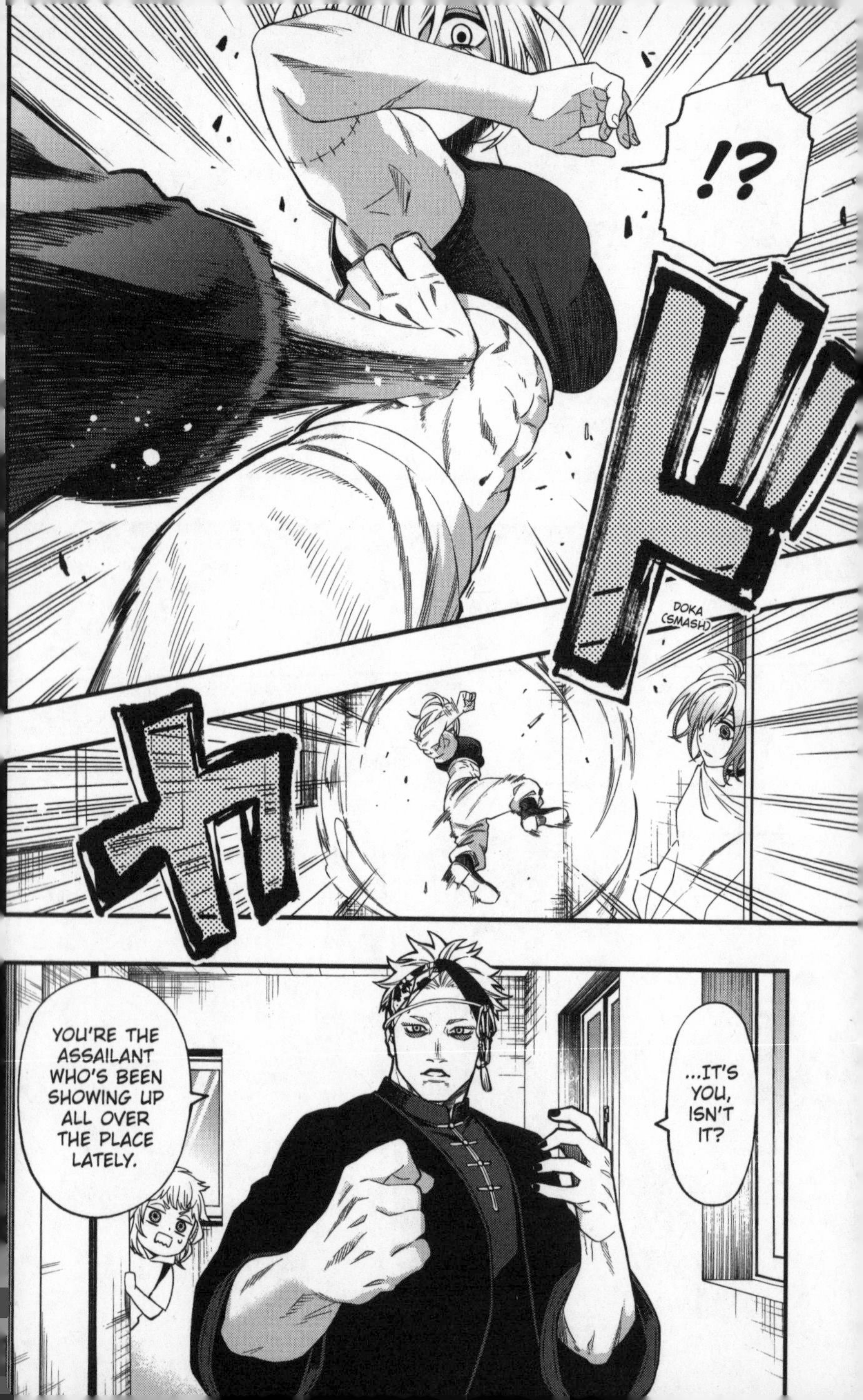
!?
DOKA (SMASH)
...IT'S YOU, ISN'T IT?
YOU'RE THE ASSAILANT WHO'S BEEN SHOWING UP ALL OVER THE PLACE LATELY.

HM...

I'M JUST ABOUT TO DO THE FINAL PROOFREAD, DAMN IT!

THE CHIEF EDITOR SAID HE'S BUSY...

WHAT AM I SUPPOSED TO DO ABOUT GETTING A TEST DIVINATION DONE FOR TODAY'S STORY?

GRANTED, I DON'T HAVE AN APPOINTMENT EITHER.

#65

AH! THAT GUY THERE HAS AN INTRIGUING VIBE ABOUT HIM!

OH WELL. I'LL JUST HAVE TO FIND SOME RANDOM PERSON AROUND HERE WHO I MIGHT GET A COMPELLING STORY OUT OF...

YOU'VE BEEN WATCHING THIS BUILDING FOR A WHILE NOW, HAVEN'T YOU?

COULD IT BE...YOU'RE INTERESTED IN PHANTOM SOLITAIRE...OR THE SECRET OF THE MYSTERIOUS YOUNG FORTUNE-TELLER?

OH, EXCUSE ME! I SWEAR I'M NOT SOME WEIRDO TRYING TO HIT ON YOU!

HEY, YOU THERE, MISTER!

WHAT DID YOU SAY...?

#65

SO THERE'S A JOURNALIST INVESTIGATING POLKA...

SHE MIGHT BE ABLE TO GET SOME USEFUL INFORMATION.

...I SEE.

THIS IS A GOOD OPPORTUNITY TO GET A BETTER IDEA OF THE LAYOUT OF THE BUILDING'S INTERIOR.

THERE'S SOMETHING ABOUT HER THAT'S PIQUED YOUR INTEREST TOO, WHICH IS WHY YOU CALLED ME INSTEAD OF JUST IGNORING HER.

Stay with her without letting her in on your true intentions.

ARE YOU SURE?

SCORE! THANK YOU VERY MUCH!

...FINE. I GOT PERMISSION FROM MY BOSS.

KII
(CREAK)

WELL THEN, LET'S GET GOING!

...HUH? WHAT?

WHY'S IT SO CHILLY ...?

ZOKU (CHILL)

...?

WHAT IS THIS?

SOMETHING FEELS SINISTER.

IT'S NOT THE PEOPLE.

IT'S THIS PLACE.

ど゛ろ
ZORO

ど゛ろ
ZORO (CROWD)

HUH?

HUH?

すん
SUN (SNIFF)

BUT...

LIKE THE CAGE OF A WILD BEAST... NO.

IT'S MORE LIKE THE DEEP, DARK SENSATION OF DEATH THAT I GOT WHEN I WAS IN THE PRESENCE OF A COMPLETE T'ING-FU.

...IT'S... NEARBY.

KA

KA (TAK)

AH, HEY! WHERE ARE YOU GOING!?

HUH?

SU (SSK)

ZUO (GWOOSH)

THE THIRD FLOOR...?

WAIT FOR MEEE!

ARGH! SNAP OUT OF IT!

WHAT IS THIS...? I HAVE A REALLY STRONG URGE TO TURN TAIL AND GO HOME...

BACHIN (SMACK)

...KEE HEE!

SUN
(SNIFF)

DO YOU HAVE BUSINESS WITH POLKA-KUN? OR PERHAPS WITH XIAOYU-KUN?

UM... SAKIMIYA-SAN... RIGHT?

WE'RE WORKING! KEE-HEE-HEE!

BUT NOW'S NOT A GOOD TIME, OKAY?

ZOKU
(CHILL)

UHH...DO YOU TWO KNOW EACH OTHER?

KYORO
(GLANCE)

OH! HUH? KOCHOU-CHAN!?

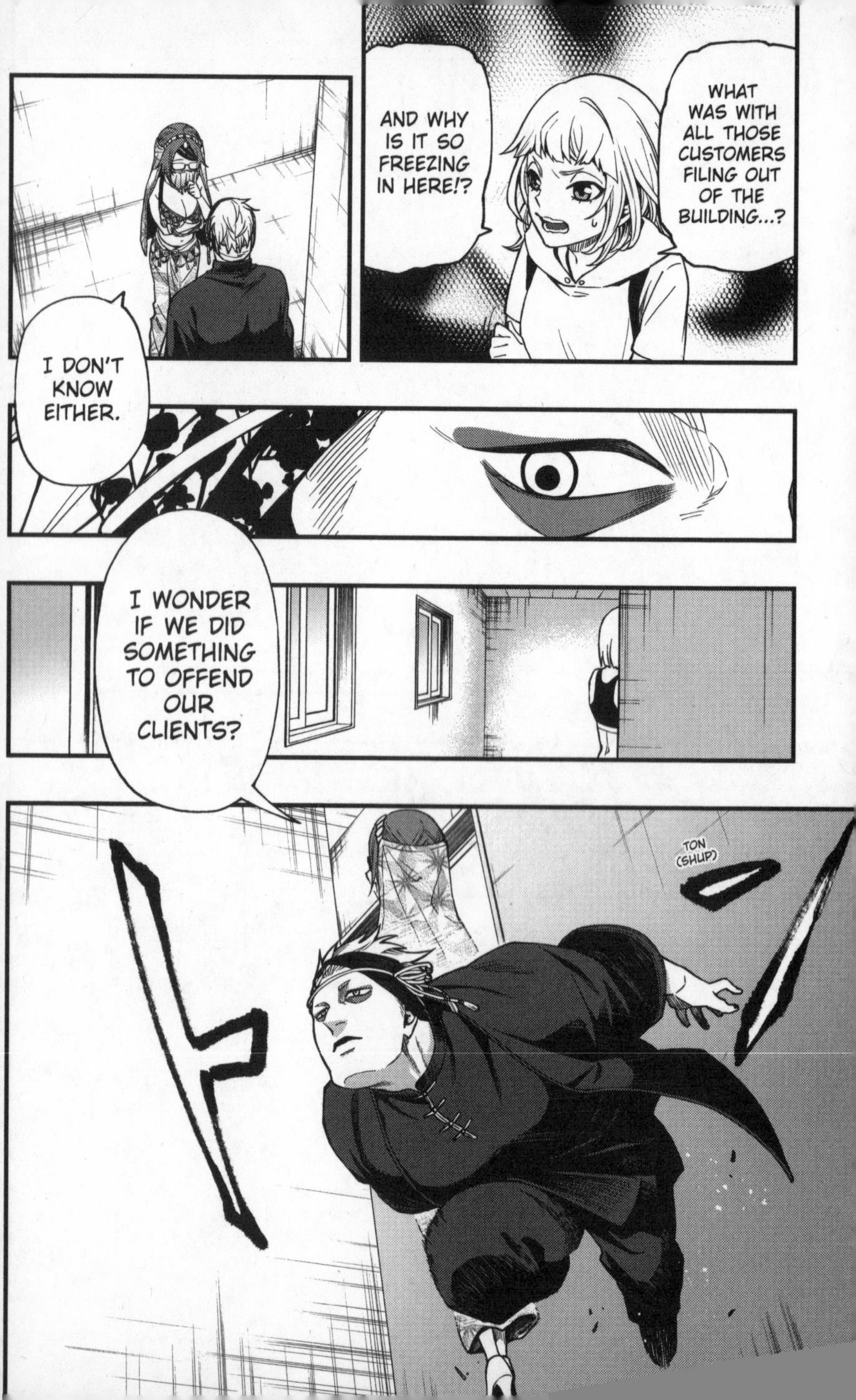
WHAT WAS WITH ALL THOSE CUSTOMERS FILING OUT OF THE BUILDING...?
AND WHY IS IT SO FREEZING IN HERE!?
I DON'T KNOW EITHER.
I WONDER IF WE DID SOMETHING TO OFFEND OUR CLIENTS?
TON (SHUP)

GUO
(RUSH)

!?

DOKA
(SLAM)

...IT'S YOU, ISN'T IT?

YOU'RE THE ASSAILANT WHO'S BEEN SHOWING UP ALL OVER THE PLACE LATELY...

WHAT THE...!? WHAT'S GOING ON!?

WAS THERE A COLLISION!?

OH...?

SOARA-SAN!

WHAT'S THIS GUY DOING —!?

...IT LOOKS LIKE I'VE GOT A SCOOP ON MY HANDS, ANYWAY!

OH GEEZ, OH BOY. BUT...

NGH...! I DON'T KNOW WHAT THE HECK'S GOING ON, BUT IT'S MY FAULT FOR BRINGING THIS DANGEROUS GUY IN WITH ME!

ARAHA-BAKI.

AND I GOTTA IMPRINT INTO MY EYEBALLS EVERYTHING THAT'S ABOUT TO GO DOWN HERE!

THINK! WHAT TO SAY TO APOLOGIZE TO POLKA-KUN AND HIS GANG!

NEED A HAND?

...YOU'RE IN AN AWFULLY GOOD MOOD, BOSS.

BUT I'LL CLEAN UP MY OWN MESS.

YEAH?

...BUT NOW THE BOSS HAS SHOWN UP?

PAKI
(KRAK)
パキ

GOKI
(KRIK)
ゴキ

I THOUGHT I'D STRANGLED EVERYONE AROUND THE BUILDING TO KEEP FROM BEING SEEN...

...TAIPEI'S MADE CONTACT WITH THE ATTACKER/CELL PHONE THIEF.

ROUND ONE BEGINS.

ARE YOU ABSOLUTELY CERTAIN, BAO?

WITH HIS SENSE OF SMELL, HE COULD TRACK IT DOWN EVEN AFTER TEN DAYS.

TAIPEI IS A BEAST.

THE CLOTHES OF HEILEI OPERATIVES ARE SOAKED IN A SPECIAL PERFUMED OIL.

IF SHE CAME CLOSE ENOUGH TO STRANGLE THEM, THE SMELL SHOULD BE STRONG ENOUGH TO LAST EVEN AFTER BATHING.

...Hmph. I'm sure.

THAT'S HIS EXCUSE.

Elimination of enemy targets who have breached safe distance from Miss Shinoyama and her associates.

...AND HIS REASON FOR LAUNCHING THE OFFENSIVE THERE?

HIS RATIONALE IS MORE BASE THAN AN ANIMAL'S.

THAT MAN...

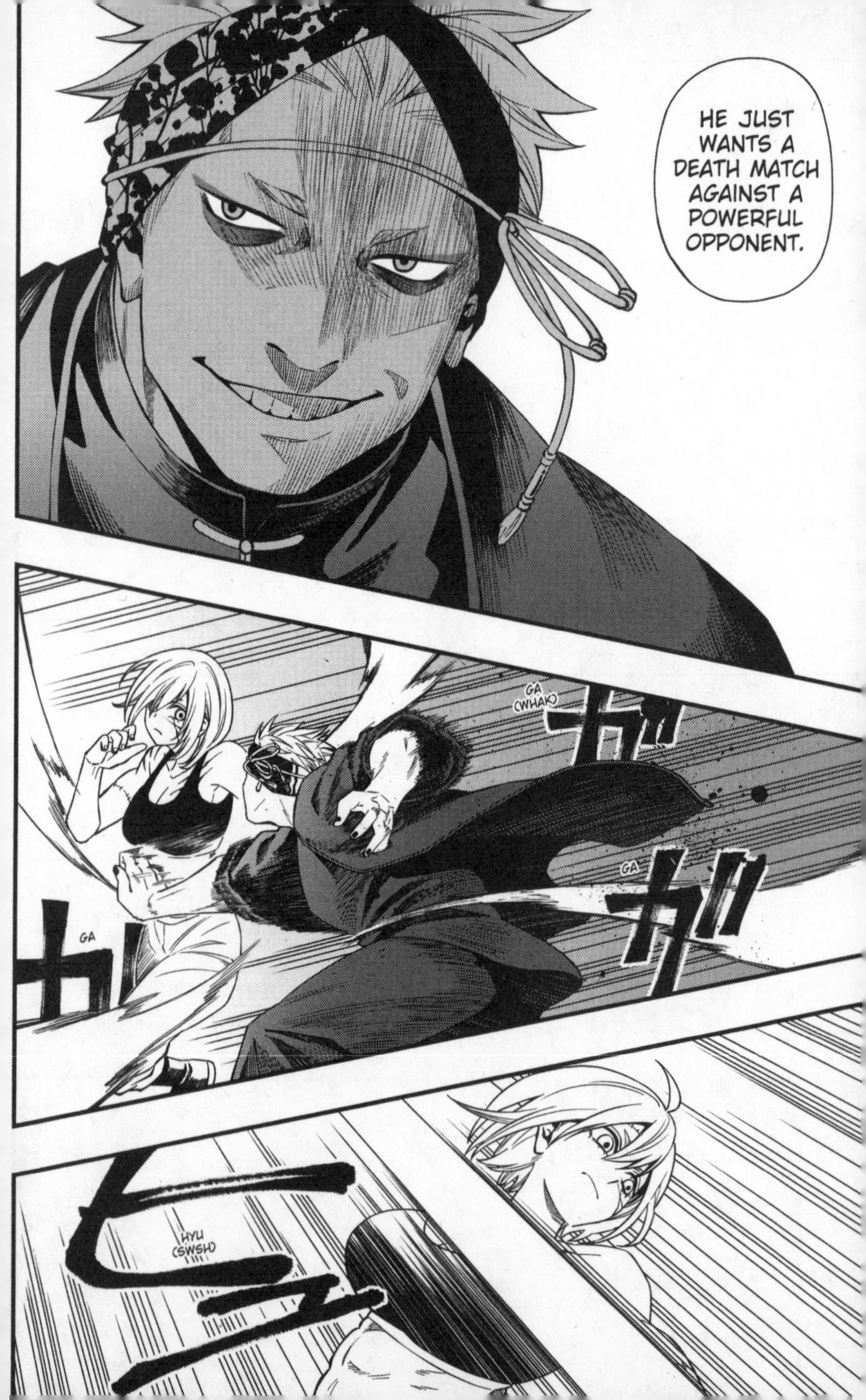
HE JUST WANTS A DEATH MATCH AGAINST A POWERFUL OPPONENT.
GA (WHAK)
GA
GA
HYU (SWSH)

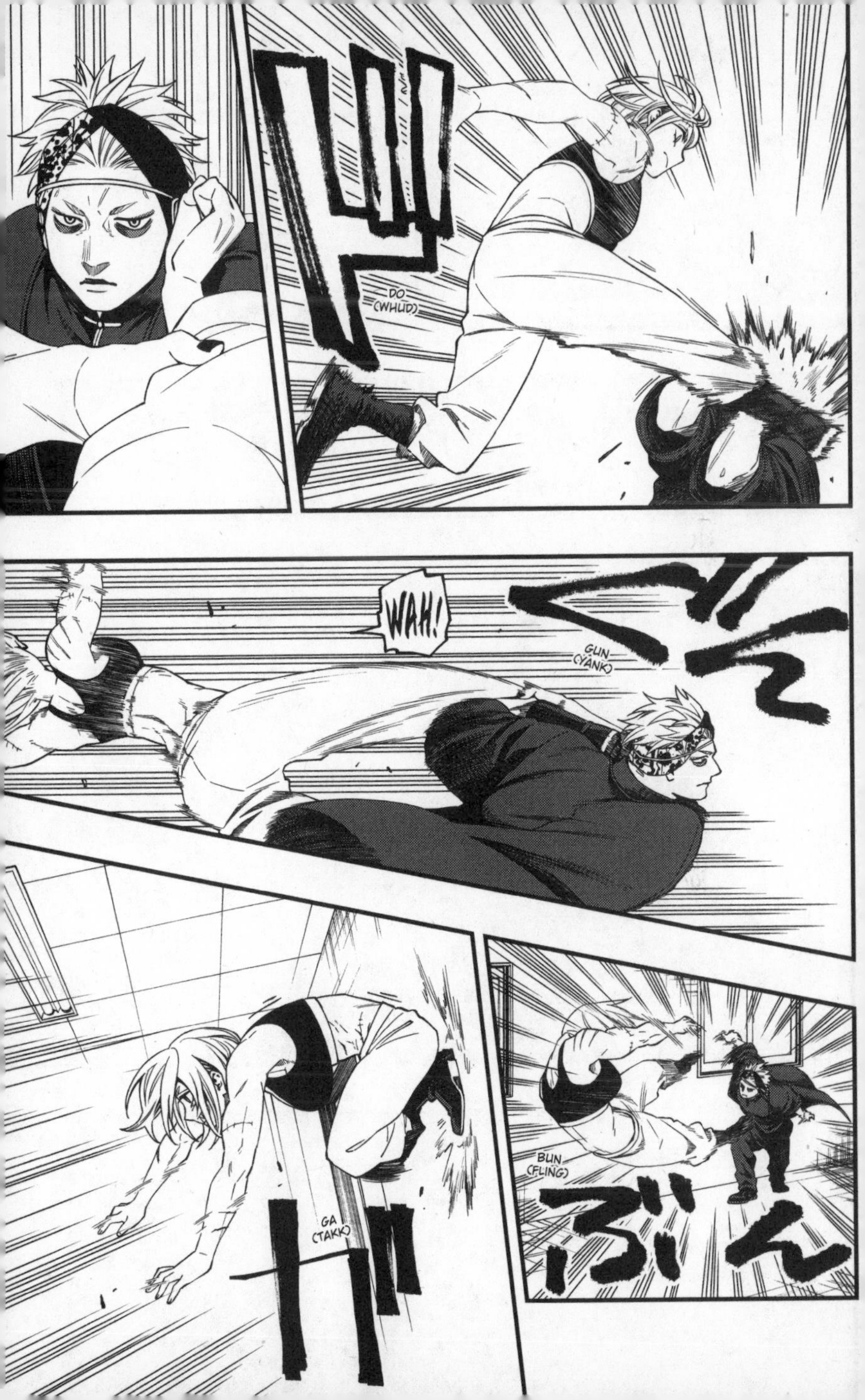
DO (WHUD)
WAH!
GUN (YANK)
BUN (FLING)
GA (TAKK)

MISTRESS! IT'S DANGEROUS OUT THERE, SO STAY IN THIS ROOM!!

HM? WHAT WAS THAT SOUND?

WHOA, WHOA, WHOA. WHAT IS THIS? WHAT'S HAPPENING!?

STUPID TAIPEI! WHAT DOES HE THINK HE'S DOING!?

UGH...!

GA (WHUD)

AS LONG AS TAKUMI-KUN IS IN HIS ROOM, WE SHOULD BE ALL RIGHT, BUT...

THE CLIENTS HAVE BEEN LED OUT.

KEE HEE. ♥

BIKU (JUMP)

ビクッ

...WE GOING TO HELP OUT EITHER ONE OF THEM?

I DON'T KNOW WHAT'S GOING ON, BUT...

HE'S UNFAZED BY THE SITUATION.

COULD THAT BOY ALSO BE A SHINOYAMA BODYGUARD?

GOT IT!

TA (DASH)

た

FIRST, GET THE JOURNALIST OUT OF HERE...

LET'S SEE...

はわわ
HAWAWA (PANIC)

THE SHINOYAMAS HAVE SOME FINE PAWNS ON THEIR SIDE...

HE'S GOOD, BEING ABLE TO KEEP UP WITH ARAHABAKI...

VUUU
(VRR)

vuuu

CIVIL-SAMA?

...WHO COULD BE CALLING AT A TIME LIKE THIS...?

Y-YES?

LULU.

...HA HA.

AHH!

COME ON, IT'S DAN-GEROUS OUT HERE! DANGER-OUS!

-ZA-
(SKSH)

BA
(FWP)

A-AT LEAST ONE SHOT...!

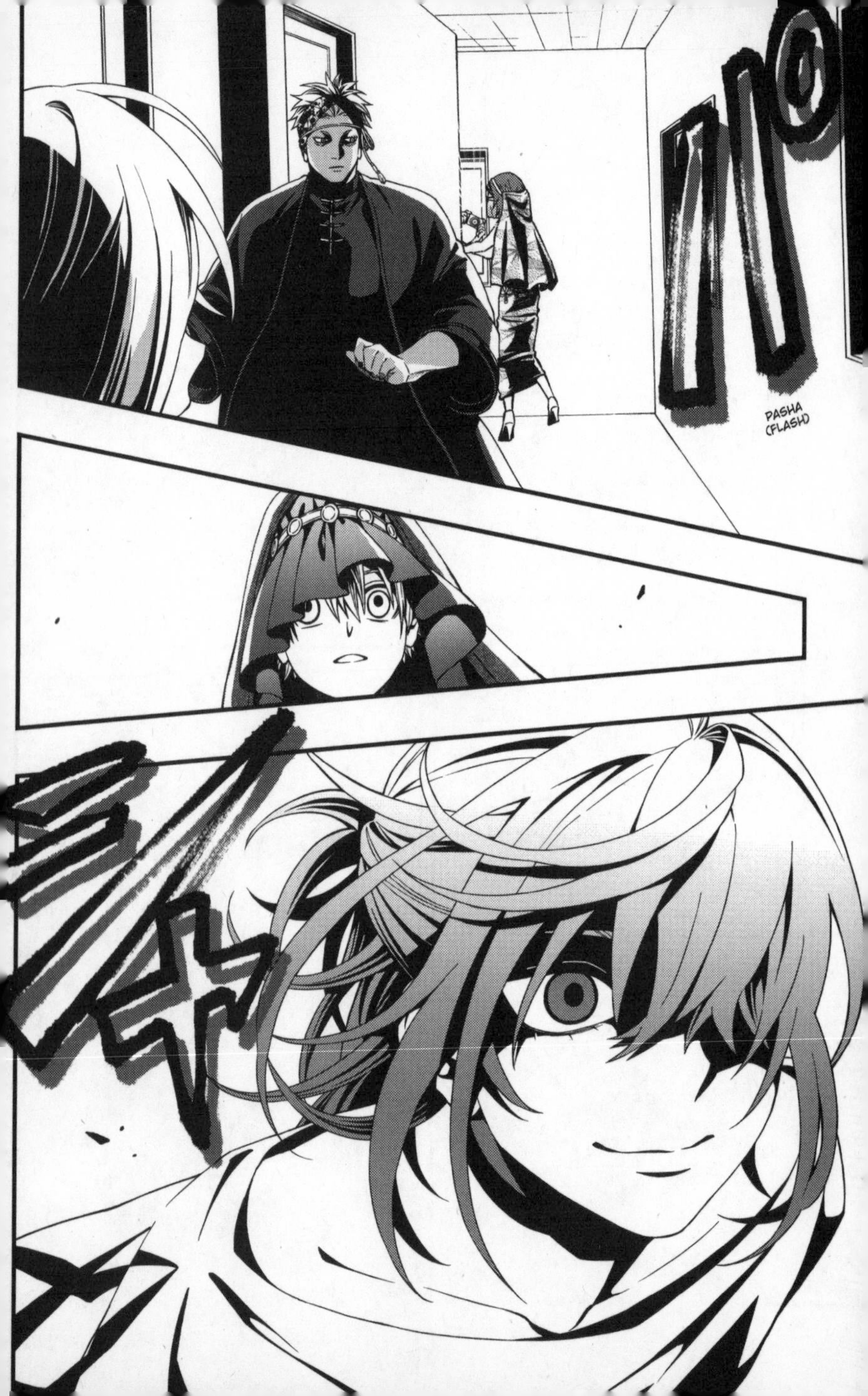
PASHA
(FLASH)

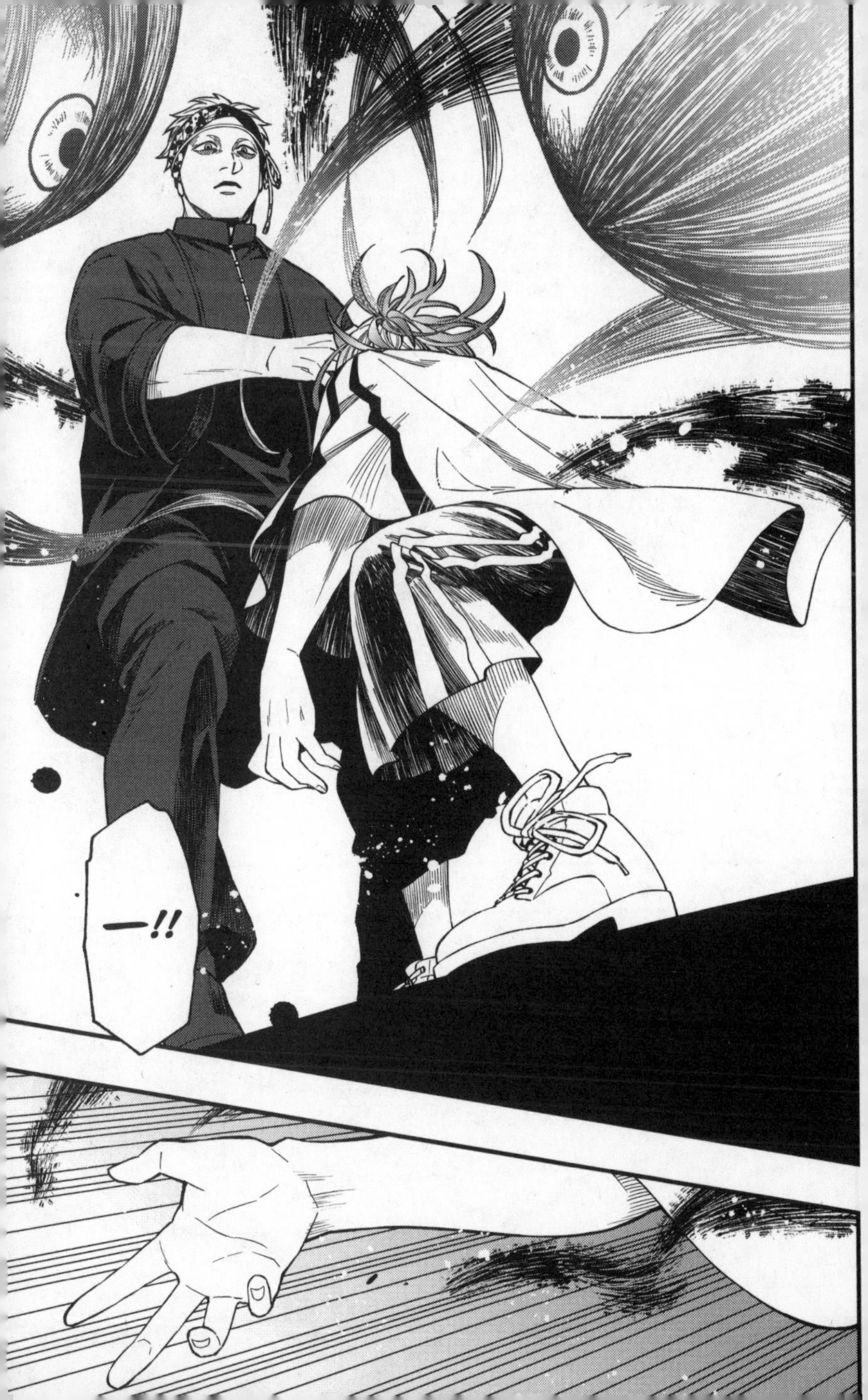
—!!

DO!!
(WHAM)

...WHAT JUST HAP-PENED!?

AND THIS WAY OF USING MAGIC...

...I'VE SEEN IT BE-FORE.

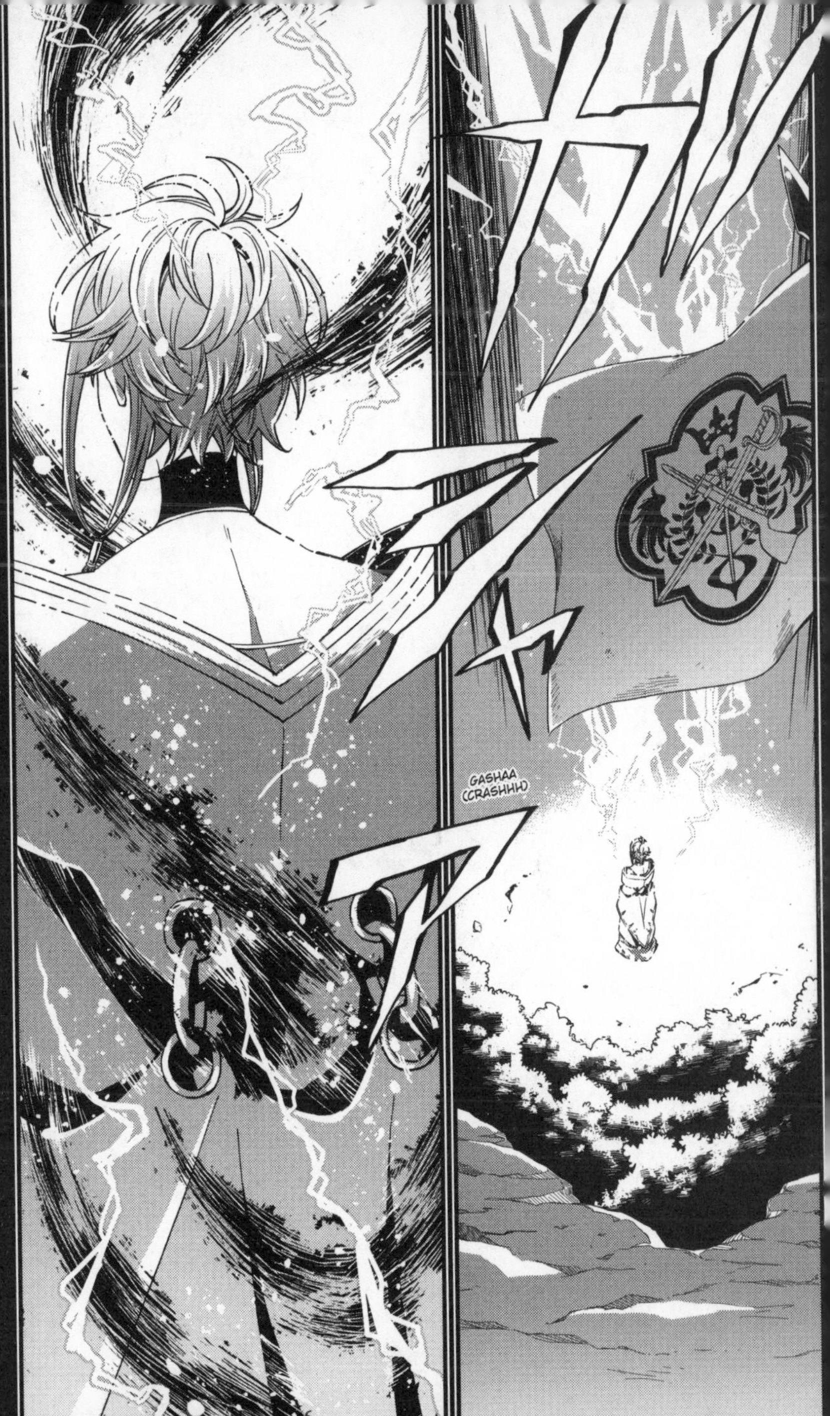
GASHAA
(CRASHHH)

!!

LORD... SABARA-MOND!?

BETWEEN A SUNKEI OR A HAKKEI...WHAT WOULD YOU CALL THAT IN JAPANESE?

PARI
(CRACKLE)

AN ELEMENTAL EATER.

GASHAAA
(KRABOOM)

WATCH CLOSELY.

...TO FORCE THE MAGIC OUT OF THEM INSTEAD.

THAT IS THE WORKAROUND USED BY THOSE WHO CANNOT SPEAK WITH ELEMENTALS
...

#66

AFTERWARD, THE ELEMENTAL REMAINS FREE TO ROAM THE WORLD TO BUILD ITS ENERGY BACK UP AGAIN.

HE DOES NO MORE THAN TAKE THE ELEMENTAL'S MAGIC DIRECTLY INTO HIS BODY AND FILL HIS OWN "VESSEL" WITH IT...

...GRANTED, IT'S NOT AS THOUGH HE ACTUALLY CONSUMES AND DIGESTS THEM.

WHEN I WAS YOUNG, I SAW MY FAIR SHARE OF THOSE WHO BURST AND WERE BOILED DOWN.

BOILED DOWN...?

...THEIR BODY WILL BE CONTORTED, RUPTURED, AND FRIED.

BUT IF THE PRACTITIONER CANNOT HANDLE THE MAGIC THEY STEAL FROM THE ELEMENTAL...

FRIED...!?

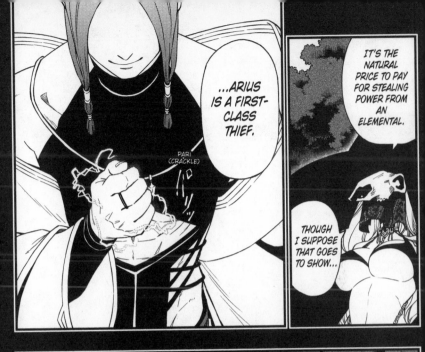

...ARIUS IS A FIRST-CLASS THIEF.

PARI
(CRACKLE)

IT'S THE NATURAL PRICE TO PAY FOR STEALING POWER FROM AN ELEMENTAL.

THOUGH I SUPPOSE THAT GOES TO SHOW...

YOU'RE MAKING ME OUT TO BE SOME KIND OF VILLAIN, IZLIZ.

HA HA...

I'M MERELY BORROWING THE POWERS CIRCULATING THROUGHOUT THE WORLD FOR A TIME.

I'M NOT STEALING ANYTHING.

?

CORPSE
GOD.

—I
ENVY
YOU.

...AND EVEN
BY IZLIZ, THE
WITCH WHO
DESPISES
MANKIND.

...BY MANY,
INCLUDING
COUNTLESS
SPIRITS...

YOU ARE
LOVED...

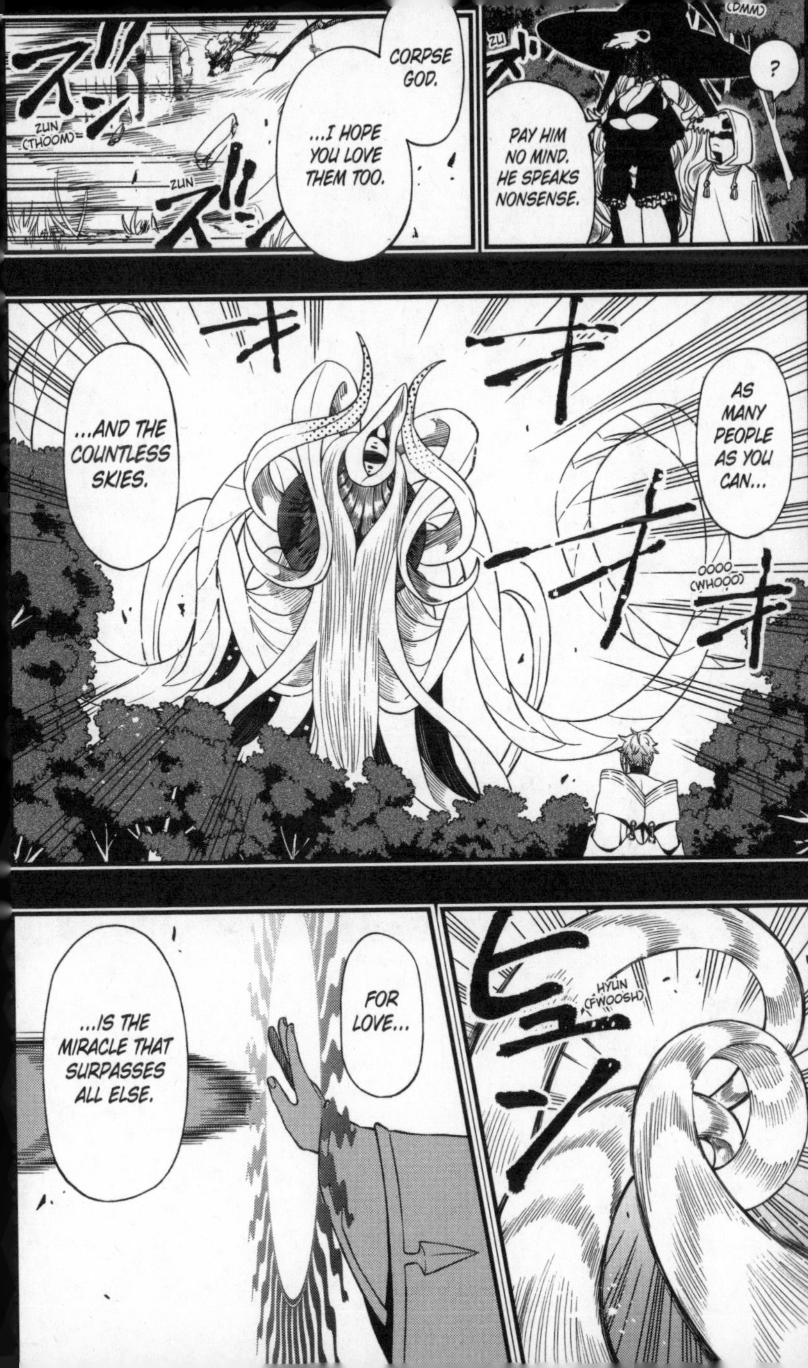
(DMM)
ZUN
?
PAY HIM NO MIND. HE SPEAKS NONSENSE.
CORPSE GOD.
...I HOPE YOU LOVE THEM TOO.
ZUN (THOOM)
ZUN
AS MANY PEOPLE AS YOU CAN...
OOOO (WHOOO)
...AND THE COUNTLESS SKIES.
HYUN (FWOOSH)
FOR LOVE...
...IS THE MIRACLE THAT SURPASSES ALL ELSE.

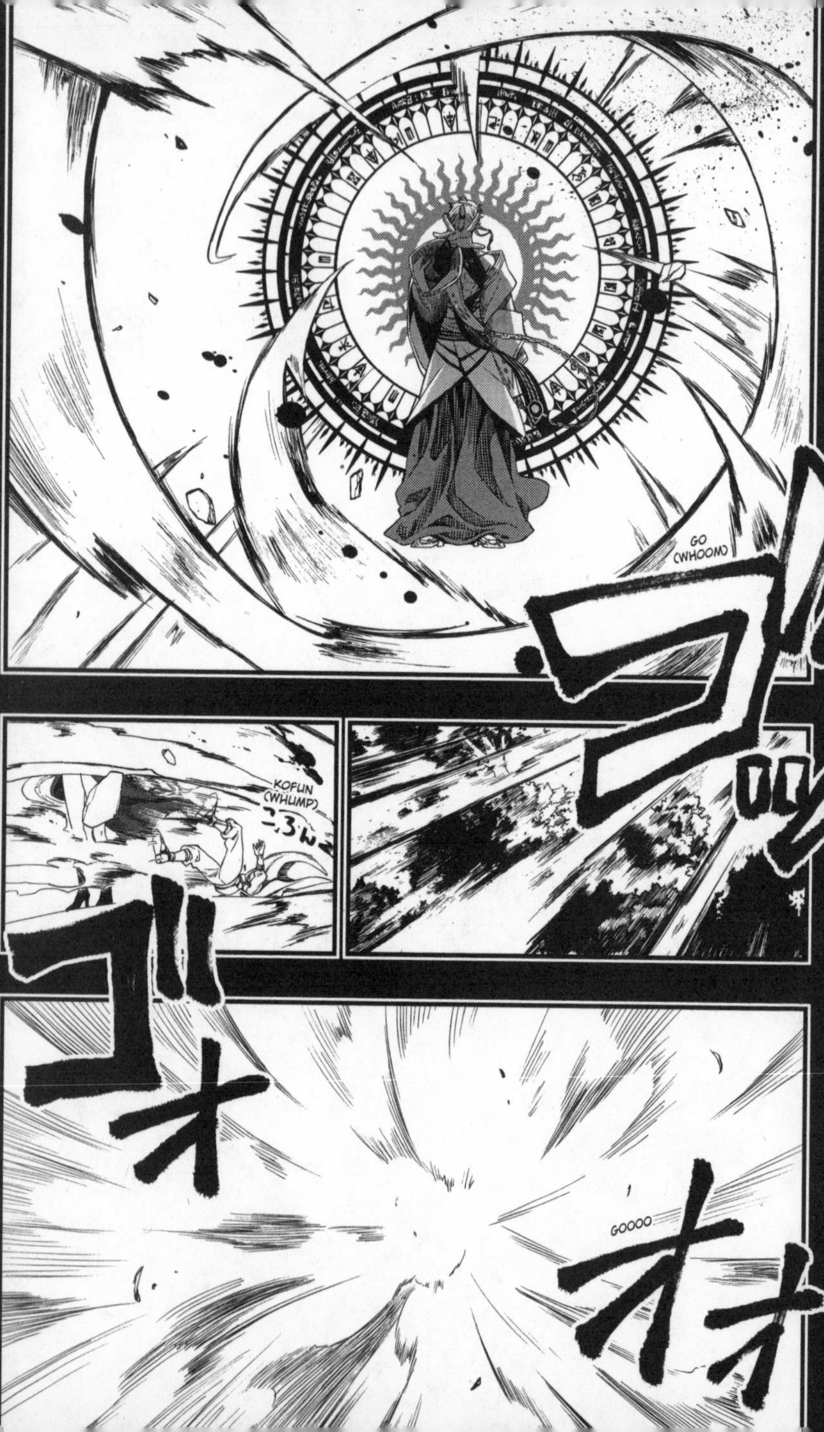

GO
(WHOOM)
ゴッ
KOFUN
(WHUMP)
こふん
ゴオ
GOOOO
オオ

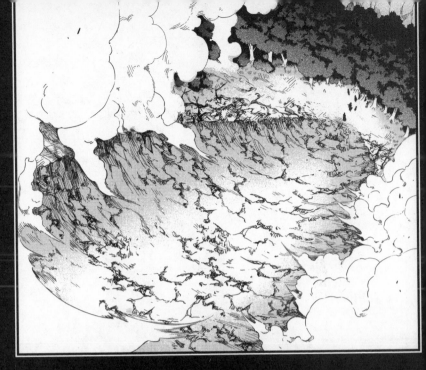

EEEK...

*HOWEVER...
I CANNOT
GET A
HANDLE ON
LOVE.*

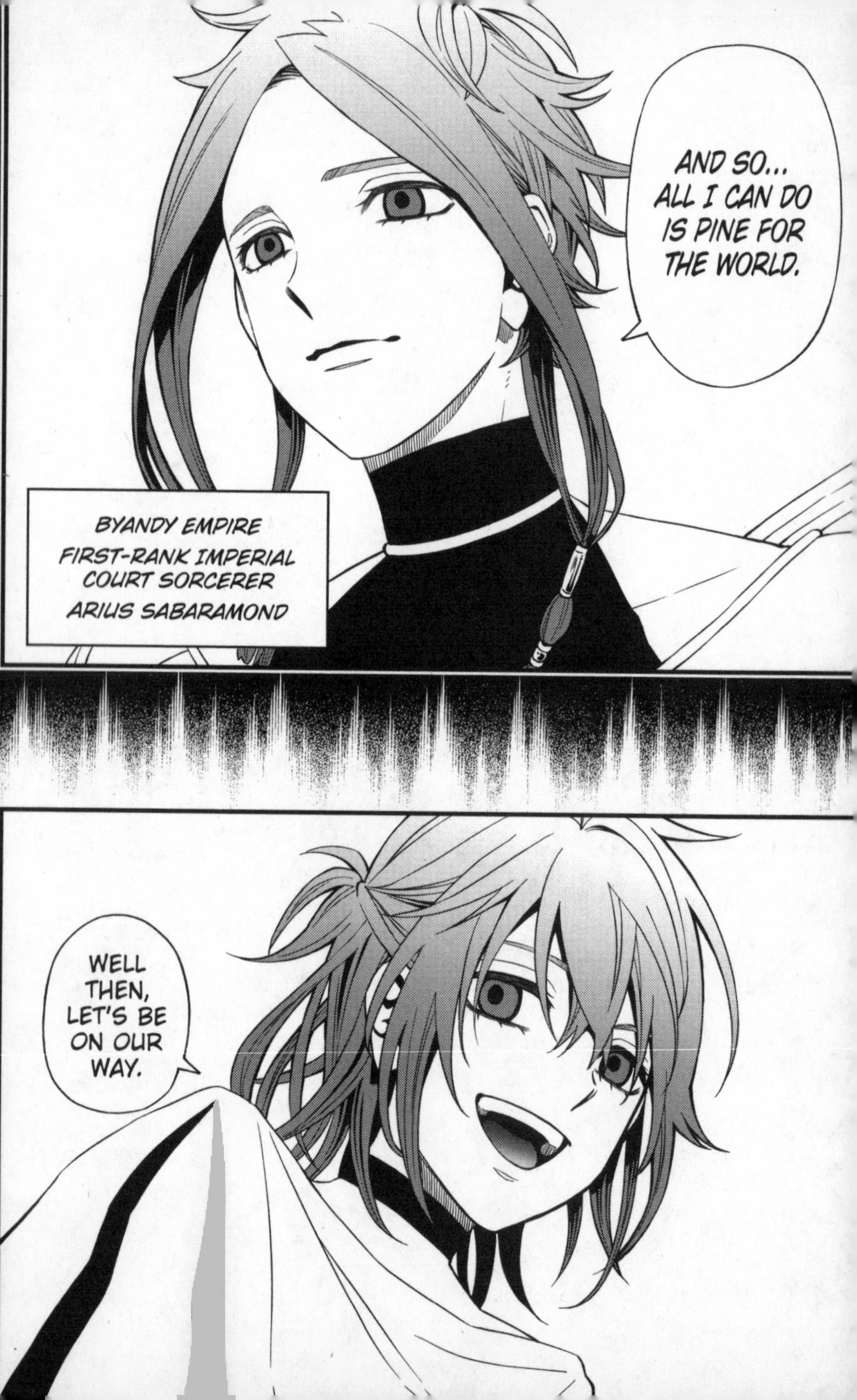
AND SO... ALL I CAN DO IS PINE FOR THE WORLD.
BYANDY EMPIRE FIRST-RANK IMPERIAL COURT SORCERER ARIUS SABARAMOND
WELL THEN, LET'S BE ON OUR WAY.

PASHI!
(CATCH)

!

THIS OUGHT TO MORE THAN COVER THE DAMAGES.

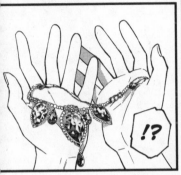

!?

HYU
(TOSS)

!!

SHU
(SHWIP)

!

I CAN'T ACCEPT SOMETHING SO—

DO
(SHOONK)

...
MISSED.

TCH!

AT LEAST I WAS ABLE TO AVOID THAT.

AFTER YOU GOT HIM WITH THAT, BOSS, AT LEAST A FEW OF HIS ORGANS MUST BE THRASHED.

ZU
(ZSHHO)

SHEESH... I WAS CARELESS.

...WHAT ?

—!?

FOR WHAT IT'S WORTH, I'M YOUR BODYGUARD, BOSS.

KARAN (CLATTER)

THIS IS... WITHOUT A DOUBT...

...THE **SAME TREATMENT** THE IMPERIAL ASSASSINATION UNIT WAS GIVEN!

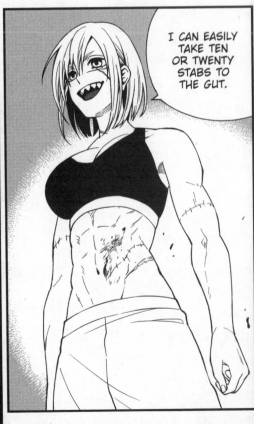

I CAN EASILY TAKE TEN OR TWENTY STABS TO THE GUT.

...YOU'RE TAKING IT ALL RATHER IN STRIDE.

YOU'VE HAD TO SEE SOME PRETTY MESSED-UP STUFF, BUT...

HMM...

WHEN I'M NOT DIVINING PEOPLE'S FORTUNES, THIS IS COMMONPLACE FOR ME.

I FORGOT I STILL HAVE MY FACE FROZEN USING THE "FALSE FACE" SPELL!

ANYWAY... I WON'T CAUSE YOU ANY MORE TROUBLE.

KARARA (SLIIIDE)
カララ...

MIKOTO

I SEE. I GUESS MIKOTO'S EVALUATION WAS ON POINT.

?

...NOT HERE.

AT LEAST...

OH... OKAY. I'M IN YOUR HANDS.

ARAHABAKI, I LEAVE LULU TO YOU.

DON'T GOTTA TELL ME TWICE.

HYOI (CYOINK)

HYUN (FWOOSH)

HUH...!?

SEEMS
SO...
YEAH.

...IS IT...
OVER?

GACHA
(KCHAK)

PROBABLY
NOT. MORE
IMPORTANTLY,
I HAVE
SOMETHING
I NEED TO
TELL YOU.

GUESS
WE'LL
JUST
HAVE
TO
LEAVE
HIM
BE.

IS HE
OKAY TOO?
GRANTED...
HE DOESN'T
SEEM THE
TYPE WHO'D
TAKE AN
AMBULANCE.

VUUU
ヴー

VUUU
(VRR)
ヴー

VUUU
ヴー

GUH
...

!

I'VE NEVER
EXPERIENCED
AN ATTACK
LIKE THAT IN
MY LIFE...
WHAT DID
THAT GUY DO
TO ME?

PATAN
(SHUT)
パタン

114

...I'M CERTAIN HE'S A MEMBER OF THAT ORGANIZATION FIRE-BREATHING BUG WAS TALKING ABOUT.

THE BASTARD CHILD OF SABARA-MOND.

...SO WHAT WAS WITH THAT CLIENT JUST NOW?

...BUT IT'S NOT REALLY HIM.

THE SHADE OF HIS SOUL IS DIFFERENT, AND HE'S YOUNGER THAN THAT PERSON WAS.

HIS FACE... BROUGHT BACK MEMORIES.

WHAT MAKES YOU SO SURE?

FOR REAL?

...WERE TOO SIMILAR TO CALL HIM A STRANGER.

BUT... THE WAY HE USED MAGIC...

...AND THE POWER HE WAS ABLE TO DRAW ON FROM HIS OWN "VESSEL"...

THE HEAD OF THE IMPERIAL COURT SORCERERS...

ARIUS SABARA-MOND.

SIMILAR TO WHO?

HM?

...HUH?

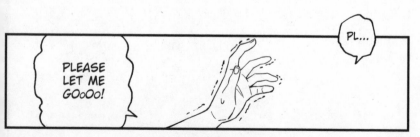

PLEASE LET ME GOoOo!

PL...

THE RACKET'S STOPPED, SO DOES THAT MEAN IT'S OKAY NOW?

WAAAH...

CONSCIENCE

AND POLKA-KUN'S A MINOR! AT LEAST LET ME MAKE SURE HE'S ALL RIGHT...!!

OF COURSE I'M GOING TO BE WORRIED...

I MEAN, COME ON, THERE WAS THAT CRAZY COMMOTION!

KEE, HEE, HEE!

WHY'D YOU GO OUT OF YOUR WAY TO DEAL WITH HIM ANYWAY, BOSS?

SORRY, SORRY.

I'D JUST GOTTEN WARMED UP, YOU KNOW?

むすぅ
MUSUU
(POUT)

SORRY I SNATCHED YOUR PREY FROM YOU.

YOU COULD'VE JUST LEFT HIM TO ME.

I JUST FIGURED IT'S OKAY NOT TO HIDE MY POWER ANYMORE.

HUH? WHAT AM I GOING TO DO WITH YOUR PASSPORT, BOSS?

HERE, TAKE THIS.

IT'S MY LAST NAME AND THE NAME SOMEONE GAVE TO AN ORGANIZATION WITHOUT MY PERMISSION...

THE NAME... SABARA-MOND.

SO IT'S WRITTEN RIGHT THERE.

IMMIGRATION PAPERWORK IS DONE USING YOUR FULL NAME.

CIVIL·A·SABARAMOND

...ARE GONNA GO WILD AFTER THEY DISCOVER THIS.

THOSE GEEZERS IN THE ORGANIZATION...

???

Have you heard of the Bastard Children of Sabara-mond!?

Hey, guys!

Word has it that the people Fire-breathing Bug has been burning...

...are friends of these bad guys too!

They recently shot at Phantom Solitaire!

They're a bunch of baddies who infiltrated the police!

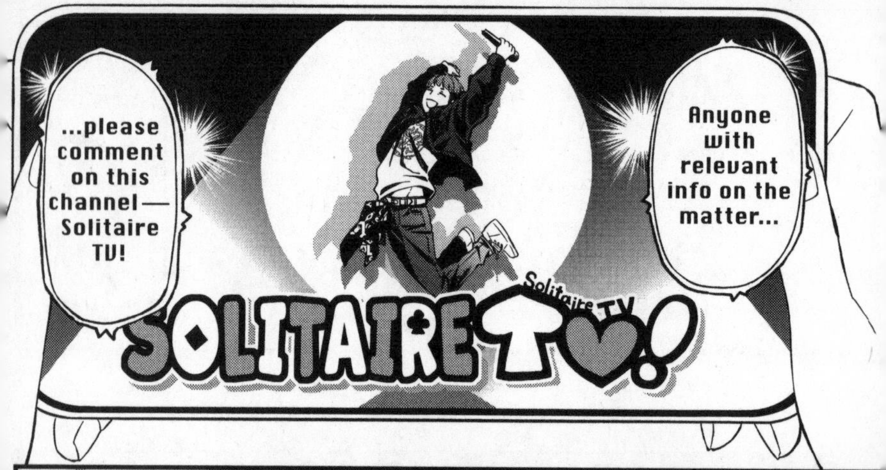
Anyone with relevant info on the matter...
...please comment on this channel—Solitaire TV!
Solitaire TV
SOLITAIRE TV!

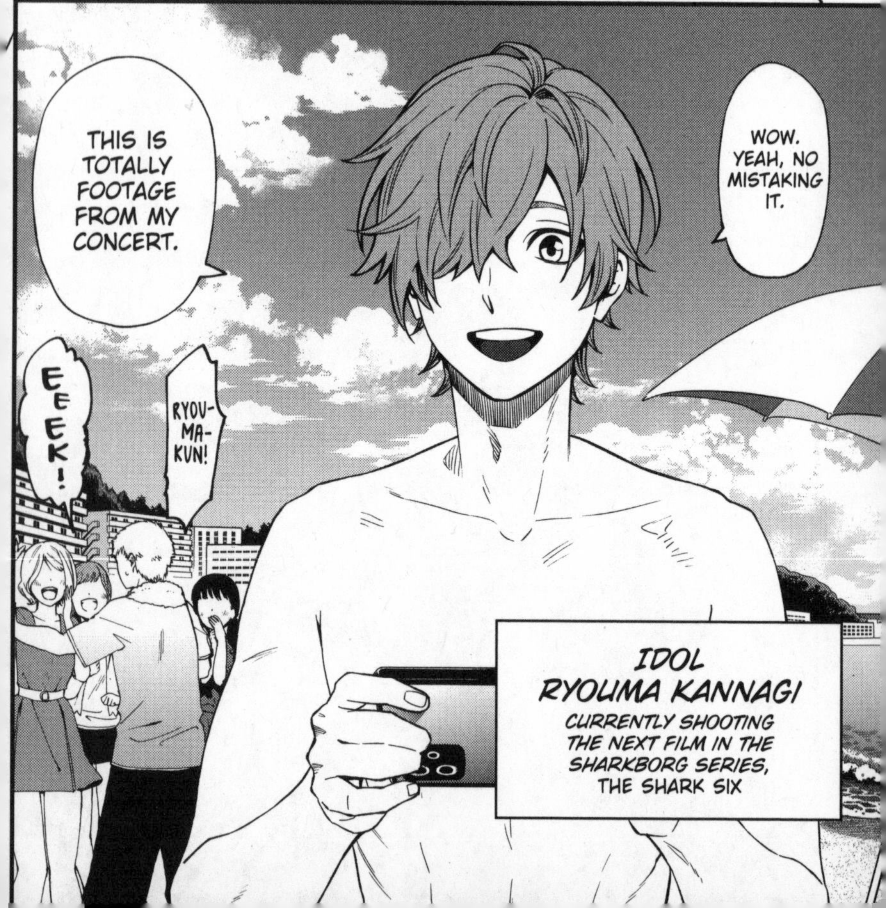
WOW. YEAH, NO MISTAKING IT.
THIS IS TOTALLY FOOTAGE FROM MY CONCERT.
RYOU-MA-KUN!
EEEEK!
IDOL RYOUMA KANNAGI
CURRENTLY SHOOTING THE NEXT FILM IN THE SHARKBORG SERIES, THE SHARK SIX

IT'S WHAT THEY CALL A DEEP-FAKE.

THEY USED VFX TO SWAP THE FACE AND VOICE WITH SOMEONE ELSE'S.

DIRECTOR

BUUUT THE FACE AND VOICE BELONG TO SOMEONE I DON'T RECOGNIZE.

THAT'S SOOOO WEIRD.

SOLITAAAIRE! HOW DARE YOU MANIPULATE A VIDEO OF MY AGENCY'S IDOL!? I'LL SUSPEND YOUR ACCOUNT! I'M CALLING MY INTERNET PROVIDER!

I WONDER IF WE COULD HIRE HIM.

HE DID A KILLER JOB...DID SOLITAIRE MAKE THIS?

AND...HE MENTIONED "SABARA-MOND"...

WHOA.

BUT WHO DO YOU SUPPOSE THIS GUY IS?

SOLI-TAIRE'S... SON?

121

Japa
1 · Manga · Trending
Bisque doll
32,334 Tweets

2 · Anime · Trending
Anime Adaptation
29,253 Tweets

3 Trending
Sabaramond
12,218 Tweets

· Trending

IT'S ALREADY TRENDING...

MY NAME BEING REGISTERED AT IMMIGRATION LINKS IT BACK TO US TOO.

RIGHT?

AH, YEAH...I CAN IMAGINE THE OLD FARTS AT HQ FREAKING OUT ABOUT THIS.

THOUGH... RIGHT ABOUT NOW, HE'S PROBABLY REALIZED HE'S LOST OUT BIG ON THE DEAL.

YEAH, IT WAS A GOOD CALL.

HUH?

I THOUGHT YOU SAID YOU WERE CARRYING THEM AROUND AS A RAINY DAY FUND.

HAAH... BY THE WAY, WAS THAT SUCH A GOOD IDEA?

GIVING THAT FORTUNE-TELLER THOSE JEWELS?

HANG ON, YOU'RE NOT SAYING...

HUH?

I KNEW IT...HE'S GONE!

GABA GYAN!

NO DOUBT ABOUT IT.

HE'S BEEN KID-NAPPED ...!!

...

I CAN STILL DETECT THE THREAD TO HIS SOUL...

BUT IF HE CALLS ME A THIEF AND COMES TO GET IT BACK...

WELL, THOSE JEWELS WERE MEANT TO COVER THE COST OF THIS TOO.

IS IT REALLY OKAY...

...TO JUST TAKE THIS?

UMM...

...THEN I LOOK FORWARD TO THAT ENCOUNTER TOO.

ごつん

KOTSUN (TAP)

RIGHT?

...YES. UNDER-STOOD.

...My apologies.

IN ANY CASE, IT SEEMS THEY MADE QUITE A SHOW OF BEATING YOU UP.

DON'T WORRY ABOUT IT.

THANKS TO THAT, WE NOW KNOW THE FACE OF OUR ENEMY.

IT'S OUR TURN TO CORNER THEM.

#67

RIGHT? WOULDN'T YOU AGREE?

KOTSUN (TAP)
こつん

BUT IF HE CALLS ME A THIEF AND COMES TO GET IT BACK, THEN I LOOK FORWARD TO THAT ENCOUNTER TOO.

SO SHOCKED HE'S...

FREEZE SHARK

I ASKED LULU.

HUH?

YOU NEVER KNOW. OUR VISITOR FROM BACK HOME MIGHT BE ABLE TO HEAR US THROUGH THIS STUFFED ANIMAL.

ARE YOU A KID?

WHAT ARE YOU TALKING TO A STUFFED ANIMAL FOR?

BUT THE ELEMENTALS SHOWED NO INTEREST IN THE HUMAN.

INSTEAD, THEY WERE CALLING OUT SOMETHING TO THIS STUFFED SHARK THE WHOLE TIME...

I ASKED... *WHO THE ELEMENTALS MOST STRONGLY TURNED THEIR ATTENTION TOWARD.*

THE SPIRITS' GUIDANCE THAT LULU CAN HEAR HAS ALWAYS BEEN ABSTRACT.

BUT NEVER ONCE HAS IT COME TO NOTHING.

IT'S POSSIBLE THAT POLKA SHINOYAMA IS A VISITOR FROM THE OTHER WORLD. IN OTHER WORDS—

HE IS UNDER THE INFLUENCE OF SOME *OTHERWORLDLY SORCERER* OR SOMETHING OF THAT SORT.

BINGO.

AND THUS, THE FACT THAT THE ELEMENTALS TOOK AN INTEREST IN THIS...

...MEANS IT MIGHT BE A CATALYST.

A... CATALYST?

COULD SOMETHING HAVE BEEN DELIVERING DIRECTIONS TO POLKA SHINOYAMA THROUGH THIS STUFFED ANIMAL...FOR INSTANCE?

...ISN'T IT STRANGE HE WOULD CARRY THIS SHARK AROUND ON HIS PERSON LIKE THAT?

THINK ABOUT IT. EVEN THOUGH HE WENT TO SUCH ELABORATE LENGTHS TO DRESS AS A FORTUNE-TELLER...

I CAN'T BE SURE UNTIL I KNOW MORE...

...BUT I'M ALMOST CERTAIN THIS THING IS A VITAL KEY CONNECTING THE SORCERER TO POLKA SHINOYAMA.

AND AT THE SAME TIME, WE HAVE TO PROTECT IT.

IN WHICH CASE, WE HAVE TO LOOK INTO THIS.

PRO-TECT IT?

YOU'RE RIGHT ON THE MARK AND YET TOTALLY OFF.

I MEAN...

MONI

MONI (MOOSH)

...THEN IT MIGHT BE THE FIRST TO BE INCINERATED BY THE BUG AND HIS PEOPLE.

IF THIS SHARK CAN TRULY... LINK US TO THE "OTHER SIDE OF THE SKY"...

BUT WHY!?

KID- NAPPED... YOU MEAN THE REAL POLKA!?

FIRST THINGS FIRST. I WAS ABLE TO DETECT HIS LOCATION, SO I'VE PUT UP A LOOKOUT.

I DON'T KNOW...

ALTHOUGH I DON'T THINK THEY'RE AWARE IT'S THE REAL POLKA-KUN...

"ELE-MEN-TALS"?

I'LL EXPLAIN LATER.

......

THERE'S A POSSIBILITY WE'D BE ATTACKED BY ELEMENTALS IF WE GOT TOO CLOSE, SO WE'LL HAVE TO KEEP OUR DISTANCE...

AS I THOUGHT... THE PRESENCE OF THAT GIRL'S ELEMENTALS IS PROBABLY SCRAMBLING MY MAGIC...

...IT'S NO USE. I CAN'T TELE-PATHICALLY COMMUNI-CATE WITH POLKA-KUN.

IT'S NOT AS IF HE'S CONTRACTED TO ME AS A SPIRIT OF THE DEAD.

I'LL EVENTUALLY RETURN THIS BODY TO HIM, SO HE'S MORE LIKE A DIS-EMBODIED SPIRIT.

MY ONLY CHANCE IS TO RESCUE HIM DIRECTLY SOMEHOW.

HOWEVER, I NEED TO AVOID FORCIBLY SUMMONING BACK POLKA-KUN'S SOUL, OR I RUN THE RISK OF DESTROYING PART OF IT...

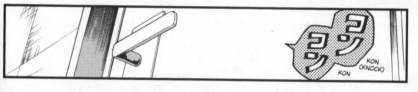

コン
コン

KON
(KNOCK)

KON

POLKA-SAMA...

...MAY I HAVE A MOMENT?

HUH?

ガチャ
GACHA
(KCHAK)

132

TH...

THERE'S NO ONE HERE...!!

TEA!? IS IT JUST ME, OR ARE YOU TRYING TO DOWNPLAY EVERYTHING THAT JUST HAPPENED!?

SINCE THERE ARE NO CLIENTS TO SEE.

MAYBE EVERY-ONE'S OUT HAVING A DRINK OF TEA!

SHOULD BE. HOW VERY STRANGE.

THE ONLY WAY OUT IS THE STAIRCASE WE WERE ON, RIGHT?

HUH!? WAIT... UH... EXCUSE US...

LISTEN! I HEAR VOICES COMING FROM THE FORTUNE-TELLER'S ROOM!

I AM SOOOOO SORRY! I JUST WENT AND BROUGHT THAT *WEIRDO* IN!

OH...

がば
(GABA
SHOOP)

KOCHOU-SAN...?

SO IT'S BECAUSE OF YOU THAT HE CAME HERE...

ER, IT'S FINE ...

ちらっ
CHIRA
(GLANCE)

"WEIRDO"...

UH, OF COURSE HE'S GOING TO MIND!

AND WHAT'S WITH THE "SAMA" TREAT-MENT!?

NOT IMPORTANT. PAY IT NO MIND, POLKA-SAMA.

IN THAT CASE... WHY DID YOU ATTACK THAT CLIENT EARLIER?

...THAT'S WHAT I WANT MY FORTUNE READ FOR.

JUST WHO WERE THOSE PEOPLE ANYWAY?

......

HUH?

ビクッ
BIKU
(FLINCH)

WAIT, SERIOUSLY? WHAT DO YOU MEAN!?

KOTO
(THNK)

コト

Polka?
It's me.

...OTHERWISE KNOWN AS THE OLDER NEPHEW OF POLKA SHINOYAMA!?

THE GRANDSON OF ROZAN SHINOYAMA AND HEAD OF SHINOYAMA SECURITY...

Takeru Shinoyama

TAKERU... DOES HE MEAN TAKERU SHINOYAMA?

TA-KERU-SAN...

I KNOW THIS VOICE...!

Those people from earlier are a dangerous group who have attacked members of my company before...

I'm the one who asked the unreasonable of Taipei and had him stay behind.

However, the damage was minor and did not interfere with business...

If you're going to write an article about it, please be sure to specify that.

!

That's right, Miss *Weekly Dry.*

ATTACKED!? SHINOYAMA SECURITY!?

...MEANING THE BOSS HE WAS TALKING WITH BEFORE HE CAME IN WAS TAKERU SHINOYAMA!?

SO THIS GUY IS A MEMBER OF SHINOYAMA SECURITY...

Well, it seems his concerns were misplaced.

The reason Taipei suddenly went on the offensive was because he feared it would be too late if he waited to act until something actually happened to you.

...I'D LIKE YOU TO DO A DIVINATION...

AND SO... IN ORDER TO FIND OUT WHO THESE PEOPLE ARE...

I SEE NOW. THANK YOU VERY MUCH FOR YOUR CONCERN.

What... did they come to you for?

But first, I have something to ask you.

......

I CAN'T DIVULGE A CUSTOMER'S PERSONAL INFORMATION SO READILY.

...I AM STILL A FORTUNE-TELLER.

EVEN IF WE'RE DEALING WITH BAD PEOPLE...?

THAT'S FOR ME TO JUDGE.

THE ONLY THING I CAN TELL YOU IS, THEY DIDN'T COME ASKING ABOUT ANYTHING THAT'S IN DIRECT VIOLATION OF THE LAW.

I'm relieved, Polka.

Heh heh. I see.

......

IF YOU'D BLABBED, I WAS PREPARED TO ADVISE YOU TO QUIT ON THE BASIS YOU WEREN'T SUITED FOR THE JOB.

AT LEAST YOU SEEM TO HAVE SOME PRIDE AS A FORTUNE-TELLER.

IT'S ALMOST LIKE.....HE'S TRYING TO GET ME INVOLVED IN THIS...

IS HE... HAVING ME LISTEN TO THIS ON PURPOSE?

HE'S LEAVING IT TO ME TO DECIDE WHAT I SHOULD TELL HIM?

!!

THAT IS WHY I WAS THINKING OF ENLISTING YOUR SERVICES.

WELL, I'M NOT GOING TO FORCE IT OUT OF YOU.

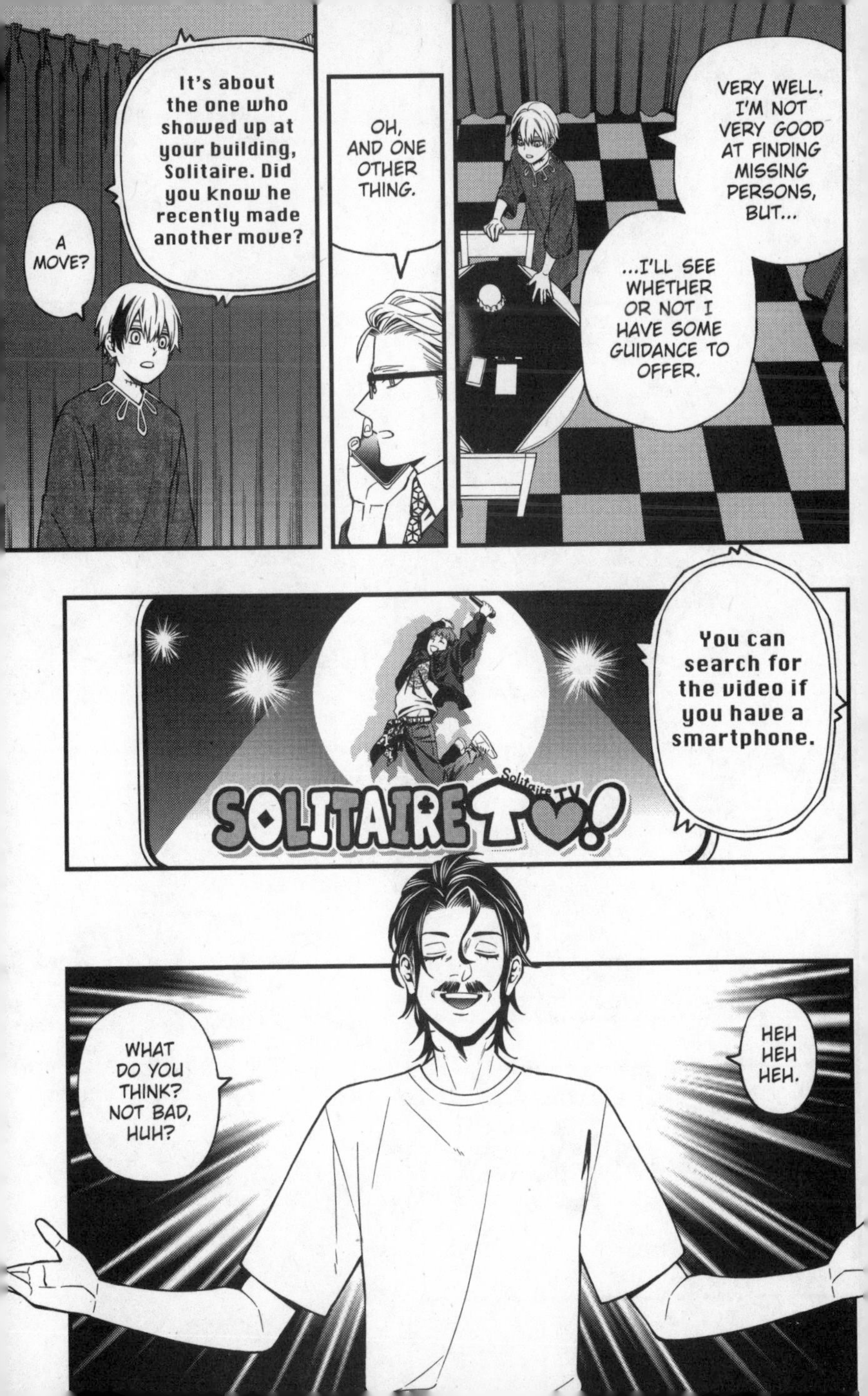
VERY WELL. I'M NOT VERY GOOD AT FINDING MISSING PERSONS, BUT...
...I'LL SEE WHETHER OR NOT I HAVE SOME GUIDANCE TO OFFER.
OH, AND ONE OTHER THING.
It's about the one who showed up at your building, Solitaire. Did you know he recently made another move?
A MOVE?
You can search for the video if you have a smartphone.
Solitaire TV
SOLITAIRE TV!
HEH HEH HEH.
WHAT DO YOU THINK? NOT BAD, HUH?

...BUT I'LL START WITH ONE.

UM... THERE ARE ALL SORTS OF THINGS I'D LIKE TO SAY...

SPLENDID! FIRE AWAY!

UMBRELLAS: WATCH OUT FOR FIRES

AND...?

YEAH. I GUESS SO.

?

WHY...DID YOU GO WITH THIS FOOTAGE?

A CERTAIN SABARAMOND GANG WILL BE SURPRISED IF YOU'RE ONE OF THEM, WON'T THEY?

...I NEED ANOTHER REASON?

ARE YOU IMPLY-ING...

THAT'S THE FIRST TIME I'VE YELLED LIKE THAT SINCE KINDERGARTEN.

SUU
(SFF)

R-RIGHT... WELL...I FEEL LIKE I'VE FINALLY SEEN YOUR HUMAN SIDE.

IS THAT... A CON-FESSION?

EVEN IF I MADE IT OUT OF HERE IN ONE PIECE, I'D HAVE TO GET PLASTIC SURGERY AND GO ON THE LAM.

THAT WAS FAST...HE SWITCHED MODES IN A HEARTBEAT!

Y-YOU DON'T SAY.

"FRIENDS"? WELL...I DO SOMETIMES WONDER WHAT THEY THINK OF ME.

I'M JUST THEIR ERRAND BOY.

THAT YOU'RE FRIENDS WITH THOSE ALIENS (PROOF PENDING), THE SABARA-MOND!

FIRE-BREATHING BUG...

WHY HAVE YOU LOT BEEN GOING AROUND *FOR THE LAST CENTURY* BURNING THOSE ASSOCIATED WITH SABARAMOND...?

NOBODY'S TOLD ME YET.

THAT MEANS THE NEXT THING WE HAVE TO FIND OUT IS...

I NOW KNOW THAT HE—OR RATHER, THEY—HAVE BEEN OPERATING FOR OVER A HUNDRED YEARS.

FIRE-BREATH-ING BUG.

TOP SECRET

...THE TARGET OF SUCH HOSTILITY FROM FIRE-BREATHING BUG...

...WHY OFFICER HABAKI'S ORGANIZATION, THE SABARA-MOND, IS...

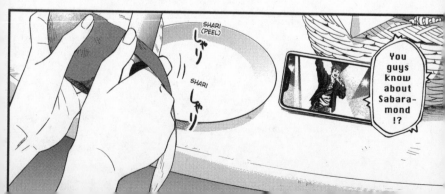

SHARI (PEEL)

SHARI

You guys know about Sabara-mond!?

...WHEN THEY DO ACT, IT'S SO SUDDEN.

EVEN THOUGH THEY'VE BEEN SMOLDERING AND DOING NOTHING FOR A HUNDRED YEARS...

THOSE CHILDREN HAVE PROBABLY CAUGHT ON BY NOW...

?

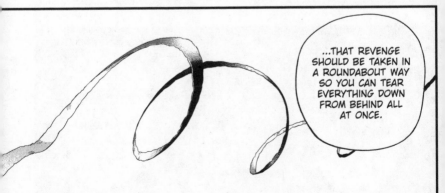

...THAT REVENGE SHOULD BE TAKEN IN A ROUNDABOUT WAY SO YOU CAN TEAR EVERYTHING DOWN FROM BEHIND ALL AT ONCE.

IN WHICH CASE, I'LL ACT TOO.

LET'S DANCE.

...AND OUR NEW FAMILY MEMBER, MISAKI-CHAN.

WE'LL WELCOME MY LITTLE KIDSASSIN ...

SO YOU'VE BEEN BURNING THINGS...FOR A HUNDRED YEARS?

UMBRELLA: WATCH OUT FOR FIRES

THEN THAT MEANS WHOEVER'S ORGANIZING YOU LOT MUST BE OVER A HUNDRED YEARS OLD, RIGHT?

YOU ARE WRONG.

HM ...?

BUT I'M LESS INTERESTED IN AGING TREATMENTS AND MORE INTERESTED IN CONCRETE EVIDENCE OF GHOSTS, UFOs, AND THE FAE...

EVEN IF IMMORTALITY IS IMPOSSIBLE, WE LIVE IN AN AGE WHERE WE GO TO GREAT LENGTHS TO ACHIEVE "PERPETUAL YOUTH."

WELL, THERE ARE PEOPLE WHO LIVE THAT LONG, AND NOWADAYS, THEY'RE MAKING GREAT ADVANCEMENTS IN SLOWING THE EFFECTS OF AGING.

...NOT...

WE ARE...

...ANY-WHERE.

...AT THIS POINT...

BECAUSE OF THIS, WE ARE...

BUGS.

NON-EXISTENT BURN MARKS.

WE ARE NOT MEANT TO EXIST.

BUGS.

...ERRORS.

FLAWS.

150

...THE BASTARD CHILDREN.

THE SAME AS...

...THAN "INSECTS" SCORCHED INTO THE WORLD.

WE ARE NOTHING MORE...

#68

THIS MATERIAL IS OVER A HUNDRED YEARS OLD, BUT...

OH! GOOD WORK, KAYAKUSA!

...I FOUND A CASE THAT RESEMBLES THIS ONE.

THE OLDEST FIRE-BREATHING BUG INCIDENT?

NO... IT'S AN ARSON CASE FROM WELL BEFORE THAT.

...I FIGURED WHATEVER DRIVES HIS REVENGE MIGHT HAVE TO DO WITH FIRE AT ITS ROOT.

ASSUMING FIRE-BREATHING BUG'S USE OF FIRE SEEMS TO BE MORE THAN A SICK FASCINATION...

WHAT'S THAT, KAYA-CHAN?

SO WHAT HAVE WE GOT?

A FIRE IN SHINJUKU A HUNDRED YEARS AGO...?

IT'S TOO TIGHT.

BUTTON YOUR TOP PROPERLY.

...WE MIGHT'VE HIT THE JACKPOT HERE.

IT'S ODD.

YOU'D THINK THAT GIVEN OUR LINE OF WORK, WE'D HAVE HEARD ABOUT SUCH A SERIOUS FIRE...

HALF OF THEM WERE BELIEVED TO BE YOUNG CHILDREN... DISGUSTING.

SIXTEEN BODIES WERE FOUND IN THE CHARRED RUINS OF WHAT APPEARED TO BE MULTIPLE JOINED JAIL CELLS.

...THIS WAS IN THE POLICE RECORDS, BUT WAS IT REPORTED IN THE MEDIA BACK THEN?

THIS IS THE FIRST I'VE HEARD OF IT TOO. I THOUGHT I'D MEMORIZED ALL MAJOR INCIDENTS IN SHINJUKU INVOLVING TROUBLEMAKERS.

ARASE AND I WILL LOOK INTO THIS HIGURO WHO HABAKI WAS IN TOUCH WITH—

YES, SIR!

I WANT YOU TO SCAVENGE ANY NEWSPAPERS AND MAJOR MAGAZINES FROM THE TIME.

WHAT'S THE MATTER?

SERIOUSLY, WHAT'S GOTTEN INTO YOU!?

ARE YOUR FACE MUSCLES ON THE FRITZ!?

HAAH...

GIRII
(GRIIIT)

NITAA
(GRIN)

154

ARASE...?

IT LOOKS LIKE THERE IS A CONNECTION...

MY EMOTIONS JUST MALFUNCTIONED FOR A MOMENT.

NO, SORRY.

...BETWEEN SOLITAIRE AND THAT ORGANIZATION.

IT MAY TAKE SOME TIME TO REBOOT THEM.

JUST ONE MOMENT... MY EMOTIONS MADE A FUNNY NOISE WHEN THEY CRASHED.

...HAS HE STILL NOT MADE CONTACT WITH THOSE THREE?

THANK YOU VERY MUCH.

I KNEW SOLITAIRE WAS SEARCHING FOR SABARAMOND TOO, BUT...

WHO IS THIS GUY?

......

...THEN IT WILL BECOME IMPOSSIBLE TO TELL WHETHER SOMEONE CLAIMING THAT NAME IS REAL OR AN IMPOSTOR...

IF THE WORD "SABARAMOND" IS WIDELY KNOWN...

...BUT WE'LL PUT THAT ASIDE FOR NOW.

...I CAN'T BEGIN TO UNDERSTAND SOLITAIRE'S BEHAVIOR...

I DON'T UNDERSTAND... WHAT ARE YOU THINKING, PHANTOM SOLITAIRE?

ACHOO!

ANSWER: HE HAS NO PLAN.

156

HOW ABOUT WE MEET AGAIN IN THE EVENING... THREE DAYS FROM NOW?

AS FOR YOUR REQUEST... IDENTIFYING THE NATURE OF THOSE PERSONS YET AT LARGE...

...WILL REQUIRE SERIOUS PREPARATION.

SO HE'S SAYING HE'LL HAVE TO MAKE SOME KIND OF ARRANGEMENT BEFORE HE'LL RELEASE INFORMATION ABOUT THEM TO ME?

I WONDER IF THE PARTY IN QUESTION SAID SOMETHING TO HIM...OR THREATENED HIM.........

HM...

OR MAYBE HE'S SAYING HE MEANS TO ARRANGE SOME KIND OF PRIVATE BARGAIN WITH THAT FOREIGNER ...?

OF COURSE, IT'S POSSIBLE THAT HE'S REALLY JUST HESITANT... ABOUT THE PROFESSIONAL ETHICS INVOLVED.

とん
とん
TON (TAP)
TON

STEP-GRAND-MOTHER KANON?

...COULD THIS BE ABOUT HIS ACTUAL MOTHER—

IF POLKA AIMS TO BARGAIN WITH A FOREIGN PARTY, THEN...

...MAYBE IT WAS TOO MUCH TO ASK AFTER ALL.

If so, as long as Little Miss Journalist here wants to go ahead with it, then I'm fine with it too.

WHAT!?

...By the way, Taipei, weren't you about to have your fortune told for a magazine article?

WHICH MEANS THE MARK ON SOLITAIRE'S AIRSHIP FLEET IS ALSO......!?

SOLITAIRE SHOWED UP AT THIS BUILDING.

AND IF SOLITAIRE'S LAST VIDEO IS TO BE BELIEVED, THE SABARAMOND ORGANIZATION IS INVOLVED AS WELL.

THEN AGAIN, THAT MIGHT BE PERFECT.

HE'S TURNING THE CHOICE OVER TO ME!?

OR PERHAPS TO THE SHINOYAMA FAMILY?

THEY'RE ALL CON-NECTED BY THIS BUILDING.

YES. THAT WORKS FOR ME!

I WANT THE TIME TO LOOK INTO ALL THIS TOO...!

UNDERSTOOD. I'LL BE HERE THEN...

SO. WHAT DO YOU SAY TO SIX P.M. THREE DAYS FROM NOW?

See you around, Polka.

OH... YES, SIR.

If we're done talking, then I'll take my leave now.

THAT DAY IS... HMM?

......

...AS YOU WISH.

Sorry to have put so much on you, Taipei.

Return to the office for now so we can have your injuries checked out.

160

BAO, JUST IN CASE, I WANT YOU TO MONITOR POLKA'S MOVEMENTS FOR THE NEXT THREE DAYS.

I DON'T MIND IF YOU INSTALL A LISTENING DEVICE ON HIS PHONE.

Yes?

Roger.

TA (TAP)

YES, SIR.

YO-CHIGI.

I'LL LEAVE SAYO TO GRANDFATHER'S BODYGUARDS.

LET'S SEE...

...IT'S VITAL THAT WE FIND OUT WHATEVER IT IS THEY'RE AFTER... AS SOON AS POSSIBLE.

REGARDLESS OF WHETHER I CAN GET INFO OUT OF POLKA...

DON'T MAKE ANY MOVES. JUST GET A FIX ON THEIR COMINGS AND GOINGS.

FIND ME THE THREE PEOPLE WHO THE HEILEI ARE MONITORING.

YES, SIR.

...THEY MAY MAKE USEFUL PAWNS FOR US.

DEPENDING ON WHAT WE FIND...

NOT ONLY DID YOU CALL US OUT HERE SO SUDDENLY, BUT THIS ISN'T EXACTLY THE WARMEST WELCOME.

IF THIS IS ABOUT MY IMPRESSIONS OF THAT FUNNY VIDEO, I THOUGHT I'D ALREADY TOLD YOU IN MY E-MAIL.

AND IF I REFUSE?

CIVIL-SAMA, THEY DEMAND THAT YOU LEAVE THE COUNTRY AT ONCE AND GO INTO HIDING.

...THIS IS A MESSAGE FROM THE ELDERS.

AHH, YOU'RE PART OF THE "OLD GEEZERS" LEAGUE.

NOW THAT HABAKI-DONO IS MISSING, WE TAKE OUR ORDERS FROM THE ELDERS...

MAY WE ASK WHY?

THINGS ARE JUST STARTING TO GET FUN.

I'D REALLY APPRECIATE IT IF YOU JUST LEFT ME ALONE, Y'KNOW?

I TAKE IT YOU DIDN'T MUCH LIKE HABAKI, DID YOU?

YOU REALLY WANT THIS TO GET VIOLENT?

HUH?

GASHA (K-CLICK)

WELL, YOU COULD SAY THAT...

W-WAIT! IT'S DANGEROUS, SO PLEASE, YOU SHOULD STOP THIS...

EEK !?

WHAT'S WITH THE FIRST-NAME FAMILIARITY?

WE DON'T THINK THAT WE CAN WIN AGAINST YOU, CIVIL-SAMA, OR ARAHABAKI.

BUT SURELY YOU WANT TO AVOID ANY KIND OF ALTERCATION... WHERE A STRAY BULLET COULD ACCIDENTALLY HIT YOUR ATTENDANT, DON'T YOU?

BASHA
(SPLAT)

WHY DON'T YOU COME QUIETLY, NOW—

...HUH?

POINTING A WEAPON AT LULU LIKE THAT.

YOU FOOLS.

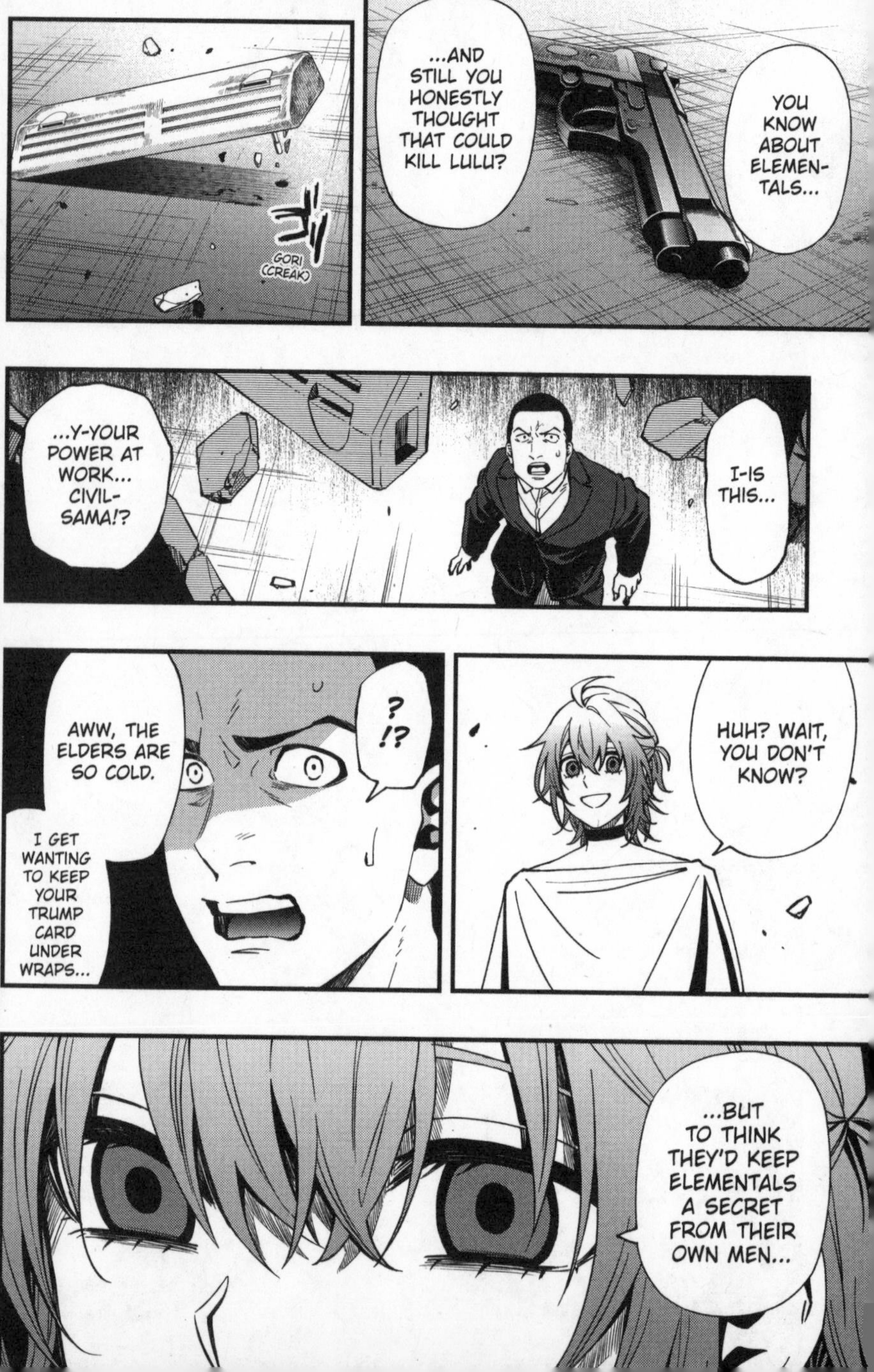
YOU KNOW ABOUT ELEMENTALS...
...AND STILL YOU HONESTLY THOUGHT THAT COULD KILL LULU?
GORI (CREAK)
I-IS THIS...
...Y-YOUR POWER AT WORK... CIVIL-SAMA!?
HUH? WAIT, YOU DON'T KNOW?
?!?
AWW, THE ELDERS ARE SO COLD.
I GET WANTING TO KEEP YOUR TRUMP CARD UNDER WRAPS...
...BUT TO THINK THEY'D KEEP ELEMENTALS A SECRET FROM THEIR OWN MEN...

THE REAL POLKA HAS BEEN KIDNAPPED!?

WHAT!?

I NEED TO PREPARE...

YOU KNOW HIS APPROXIMATE LOCATION, RIGHT?

Shouldn't we be trying to rescue him?

YOU MEAN... THE BLACK-HAIRED GIRL?

ESPECIALLY THAT PETITE GIRL WHO WAS WITH THEM.

ARE THEY THAT TOUGH?

IF WE RUSH IN CARELESSLY, IT'LL ONLY BLOW UP IN OUR FACES.

SHE'S POSSESSED BY AN ELEMENTAL...

EVEN WITH JUST THE ONE SHE HAS...

...SHE MIGHT BE ABLE TO DESTROY THE ENTIRE CITY.

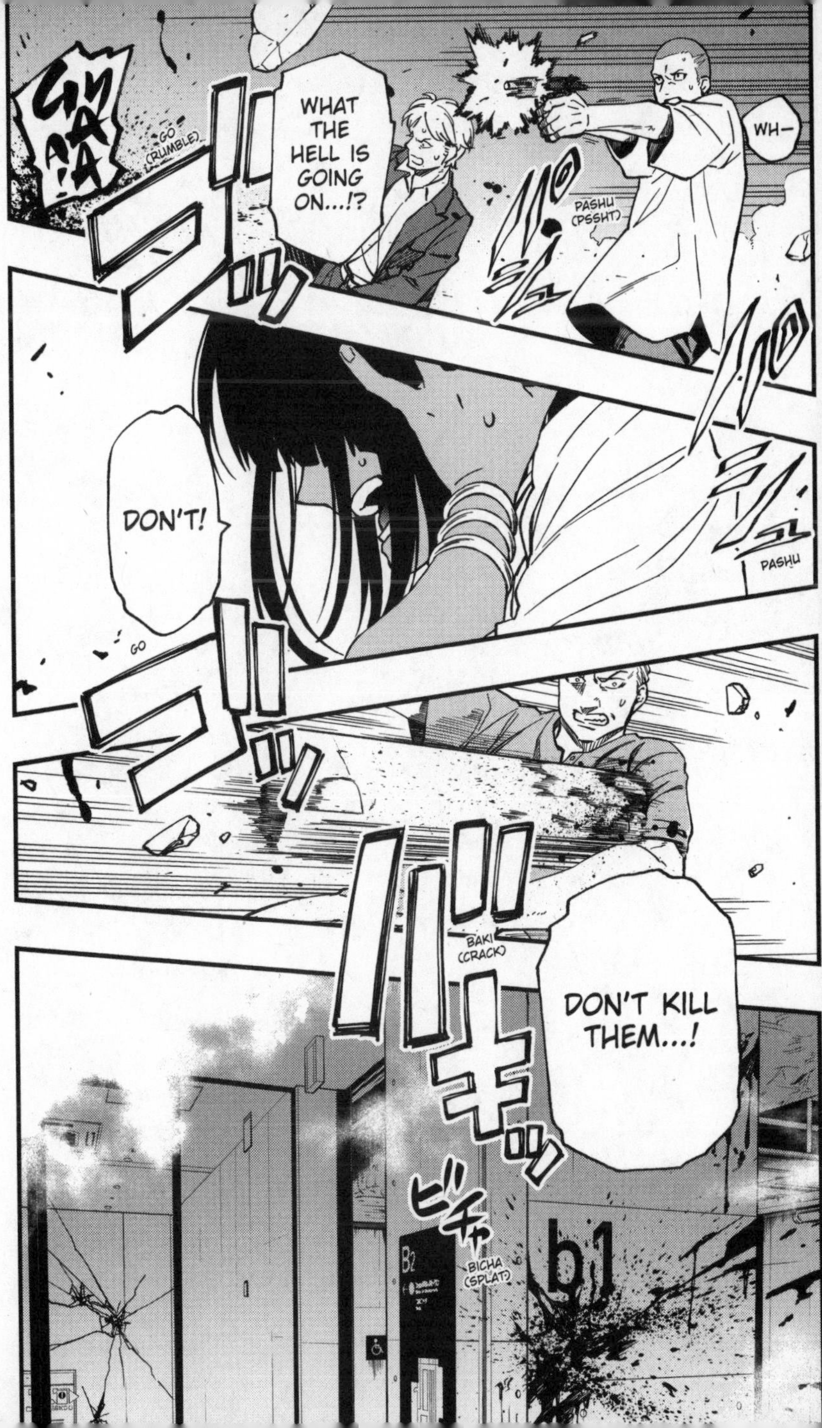
WH—
PASHU (PSSHT)
WHAT THE HELL IS GOING ON...!?
GO (RUMBLE)
PASHU
DON'T!
GO
DON'T KILL THEM...!
BAKI (CRACK)
BICHA (SPLAT)
B2
b1

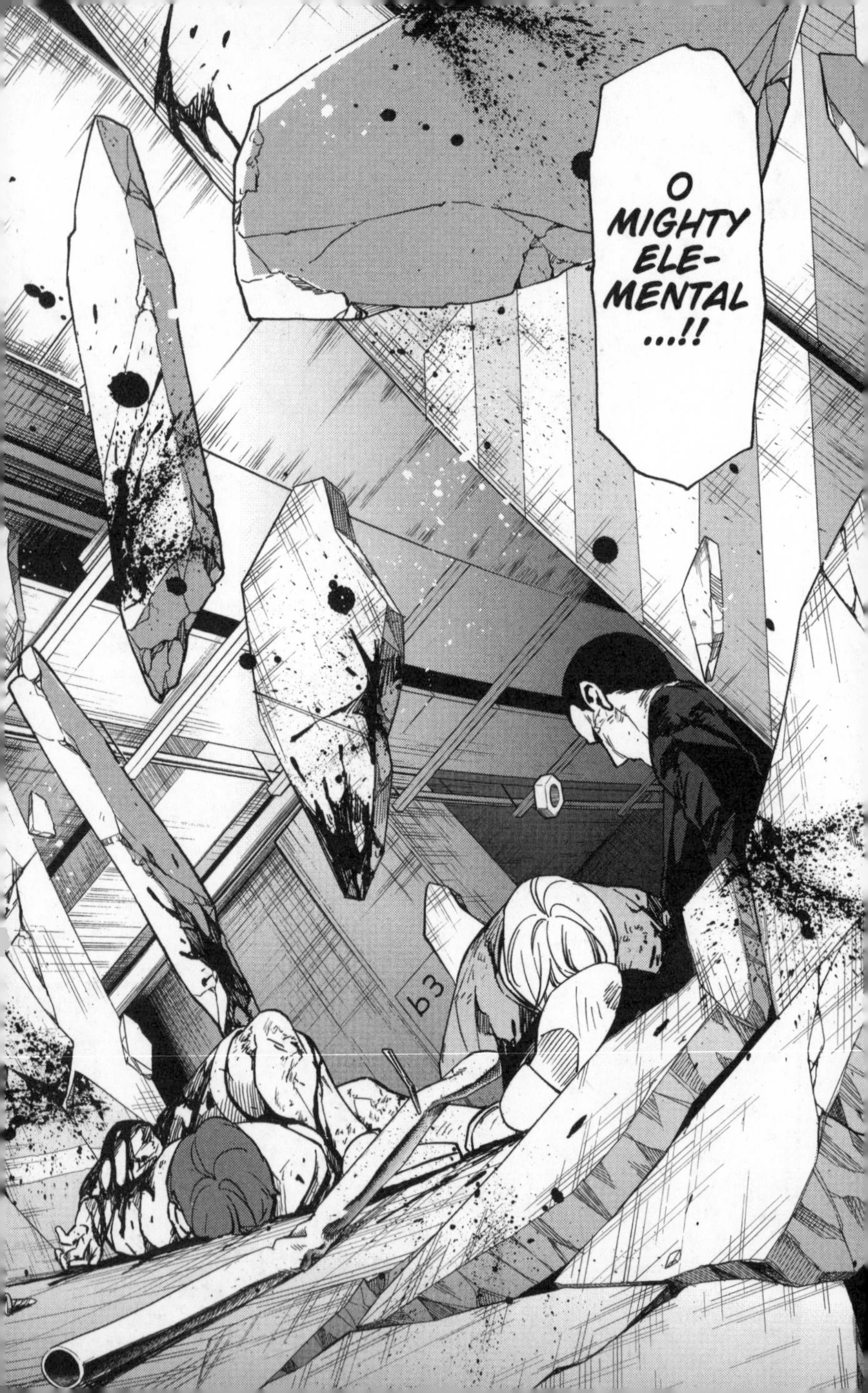
O MIGHTY ELE-MENTAL...!!

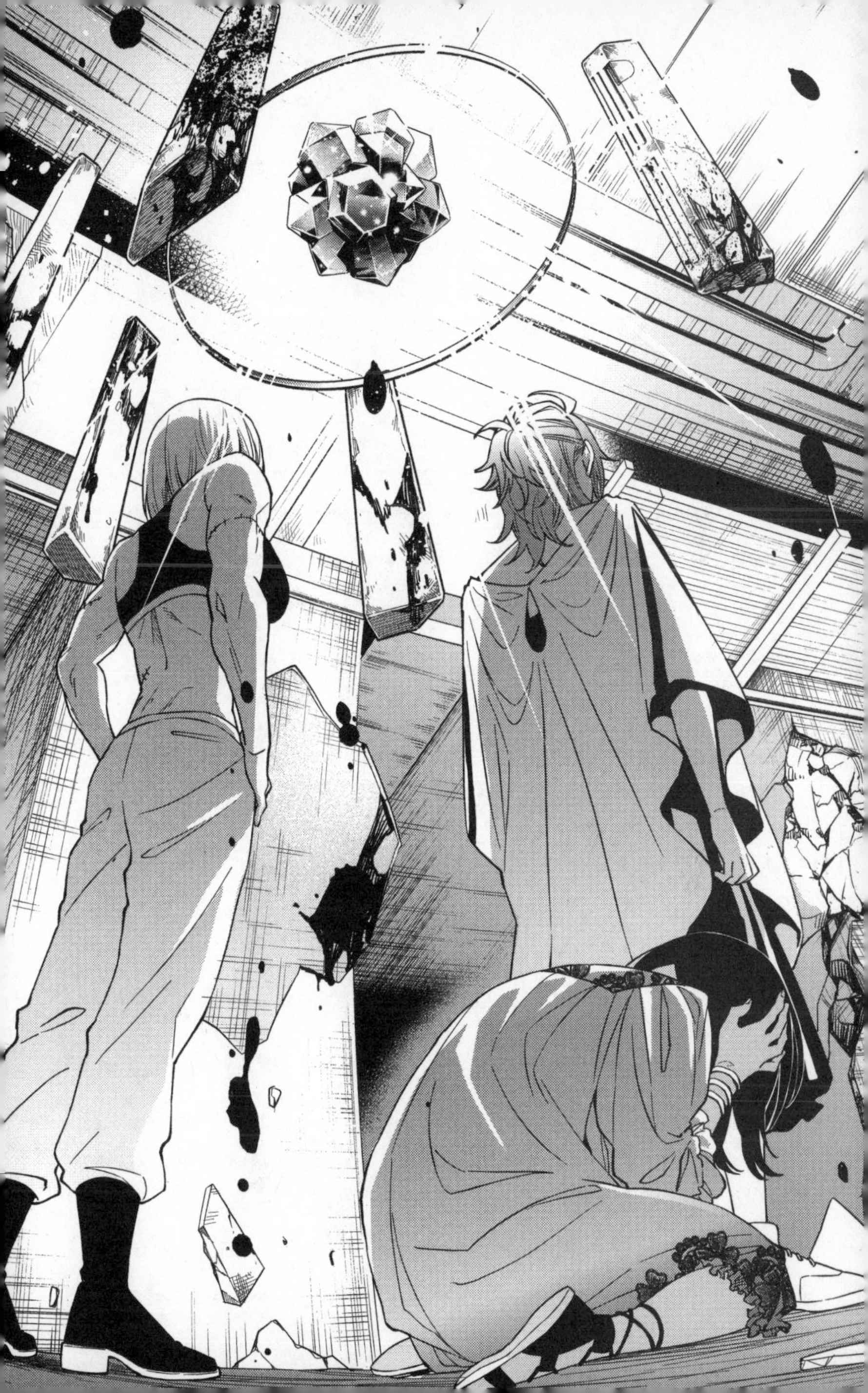

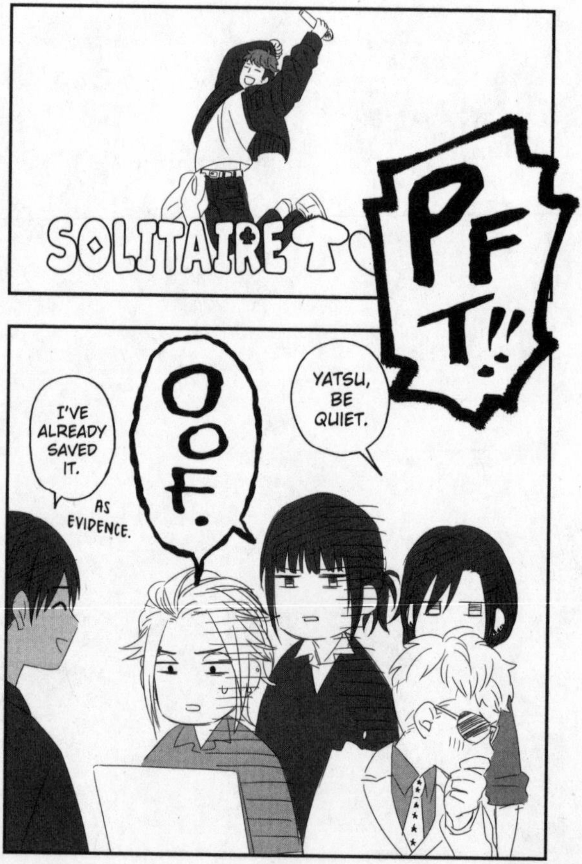
SOLITAIRE
PFT!!
YATSU, BE QUIET.
OOF.
I'VE ALREADY SAVED IT.
AS EVIDENCE.

WHAT HAP-PENED?

...IT LOOKS LIKE THEY RAN INTO SOME TROUBLE WITH AN ARMED GANG IN AN UNDERGROUND PARKING LOT.

I WAS TAILING THOSE THREE PEOPLE LIKE YOU ASKED, BUT...

Now that it's the scene of a crime, getting in there is gonna be difficult.

! WHAT'S THE SIT-UATION?

It's over.

Not least of all because I'd get a whole lot more blood evidence on my shoes than I'd care to.

#69

WHAT'S ALL THE RACKET ABOUT?

174

SOUNDS LIKE A COUPLE OF GANGS GOT INTO IT IN THE WEST EXIT UNDERGROUND PARKING LOT.

APPARENTLY, FIREARMS WERE INVOLVED, AND THERE ARE OVER TEN WOUNDED.

LIKE WE'RE NOT BUSY ENOUGH...IS EVERYONE JUST LOSING THEIR SHIT BECAUSE OF THE DAMNED HEAT?

HAAAH. THEY'LL PROBABLY BE CALLING US IN FOR BACKUP.

DID I CALL IT OR WHAT?

MANAGER, THEY'VE REQUESTED OUR BACKUP.

NO...

WAS THE REQUEST SENT TO THE ENTIRE STATION?

GET ANOTHER GURNEY OVER HERE STAT!

...WHAT?

THEY ASKED FOR COMPS-3 SPECIALLY.

THIS...IS NO ORDINARY TURF WAR.

THE ONLY ONE CAPABLE OF THIS...

...AS FAR AS I KNOW, ANYWAY... WOULD BE ONE OF THE TROUBLE-MAKERS.

NAMELY, LEMMINGS.

KACHI
(CLICK)
カチ

... YES.

VUUU
(BUZZ)

VUUU

YOU ALREADY DONE WITH YOUR JOB THERE?

NEZU, THAT YOU? WHAT'S UP?

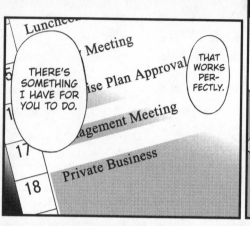

Luncheo...

...Meeting

THERE'S SOMETHING I HAVE FOR YOU TO DO.

...se Plan Approval

THAT WORKS PERFECTLY.

...agement Meeting

17

Private Business

18

...SO YOU'LL BE BACK HERE IN THREE DAYS.

CHOKON
(PLUP)

ちょ

こん

I DOUBT ANY OF THEM ARE DEAD.

AFTER ALL, YOU DID YOUR VERY BEST TO PERSUADE THE ELEMENTAL.

DON'T WORRY YOURSELF ABOUT IT, LULU.

ず——ん

ZUUUN
(GLOOM)

THE OLD GEEZERS ARE THOROUGH ABOUT THESE THINGS.

THE SECURITY CAMERAS IN THE PARKING LOT WERE DESTROYED.

AND THERE WERE VIRTUALLY NO CARS PARKED THERE.

BESIDES, NO INNOCENTS GOT MIXED UP IN IT.

NGH... BUT...

ボすっ
(POMF)

...WHAT WERE THEY THINKING, SENDING OUT THOSE GOONS TO OPENLY GET IN OUR WAY LIKE THAT?

I KNEW OUR ORGANI-ZATION WASN'T TOTALLY UNIFIED OR ANYTHING, BUT...

UMBRELLAS: WATCH OUT FOR FIRES

THEY'RE AFRAID OF THE BUG.

THOSE OLD GEEZERS DIDN'T WANT TO GET BURNED THEMSELVES.

IT'S WHY THEY'VE LEFT THE COUNTRY FOR THE TIME BEING TOO.

THAT'S WHY THEY'RE AFRAID OF ME LEAKING ANY INFORMATION.

THIS ISN'T SOMEONE ELSE'S PROBLEM.

THEY THINK THE BURNING WILL SPREAD ALL THE WAY TO THOSE OF US HERE AT HEADQUARTERS, IN THIS REMOTE CITY IN THE EAST.

I KNOW IT'S NOT FAIR TO THEM, BUT FOR US, THE OLD GEEZERS' CONCERNS ARE NOT OUR PROBLEM.

ARAHABAKI AND I CAN HANDLE FIRE.

AND LULU HAS HER GREAT ELEMENTAL.

"HANDLE" HOW?

YOU'VE GOT A POINT THERE.

BUT...THE MAJORITY OF OUR SUB-FACTION OF THE ORGANIZATION WOULD ACTUALLY DIE IF BURNED.

HUH?

SO I FIGURE I'LL TAKE THE FLAMES MYSELF BEFORE THEY TAKE ANY HEAT.

WHERE THE BUG IS CONCERNED, I BELIEVE I'D BE THE BEST BAIT.

YOU KNOW THAT PHRASE THEY HAVE OVER HERE? "RUSHING TO YOUR DOOM LIKE A MOTH FLYING INTO THE FLAMES"?

I STAND OUT AS MUCH AS A PERSON CAN, GATHERING OUR PEOPLE TO THIS CITY.

DON'T YOU THINK THAT CRUSHING THEM ALL IN ONE FELL SWOOP IS AN EFEFCTIVE WAY TO DO THINGS?

WHAT ARE YOU DOING, MOTH?

AND SMASH THAT "LIKE" BUTTON!

BEFORE THAT HAPPENS, I'VE GOT TO COLLECT AS MUCH DATA AS I CAN AND RESPOND TO THEM ALL!

I'D LOVE FOR THEM TO FILE A SUIT AGAINST YOU...

KATA (TAPPA)
KATA
KATA
KATA

CHECKING THE COMMENTS ON MY VIDEO, OF COURSE!

RYOUMA KANNAGI'S PEOPLE MAY WELL SEND A CEASE AND DESIST TO THE SITE AND HAVE MY VIDEO TAKEN DOWN!

WHERE ARE YOU GETTING ALL THIS MONEY FROM...?

IF THEY DON'T FORGIVE ME THEN, THAT'S WHEN I'LL PULL OUT THE BIG GUNS! AND PAY THEM FOR DAMAGES!

I SAW ONLINE THAT THEY'RE RYOUMA KANNAGI'S FAVORITE. IT'S THE SAME LUXURY SNACK I OFFERED AS AN APOLOGY BACK WHEN I KIDNAPPED THE PRIME MINISTER.

OH, HUSH. I ALREADY SENT A LETTER OF APOLOGY AND A BOX OF CAKES TO HIS OFFICE.

SOME OF THE MOST TALENTED MAGICIANS ARE EVEN GIFTED WITH OIL FIELDS.

I'D PERFORM FOR THE UPPER ECHELONS OF OVERSEAS SOCIETY, WHO OFTEN AWARDED ME GREAT SUMS OF MONEY AND MOUNTAINS OF JEWELS.

WHY, IN DAYS GONE BY, I MADE A FORTUNE ABROAD WITH MY MANY EXPLOITS AS *"THE MYSTERIOUS PHANTOM MAGICIAN YUKI TENGU."*

GRANTED, THE AIRCRAFT I USED IN MY "JUMBO JET TELEPORT SHOW" WAS CONFISCATED BY THE POLICE, AND THE LUXURY LINER GOT STOLEN BY THAT IKEBUKURO TROUBLEMAKER, DEUS EX KINEMA...

IN MY CASE, I ACQUIRED MINES, AIRCRAFTS, AND LUXURY LINERS AT A VERY YOUNG AGE.

PILING ON THE WEALTH!

PROVIDED YOU SUPPLY ME WITH THE RIGHT INFORMATION, OF COURSE... IF YOU CATCH MY DRIFT.

ANYWAY! PREPARATIONS ARE UNDERWAY TO HAVE YOU TELEPORTED TO A SAFE NEW LAND!

WHAT IS IT...THAT HAPPENED THERE?

WHY...THE BUILDING WHERE THAT FORTUNE-TELLER IS?

WHAT?

...THERE'S SOMETHING I'D LIKE TO ASK AS WELL.

...WAS THAT YOUR MAGIC TRICK?

THE GIANT SWARM OF ARMS THAT STREAMER CAUGHT ON VIDEO...

THAT'S A VERY INTRIGUING STORY.

BECAUSE YOU MAY ALREADY HAVE ATTAINED WHAT YOU DESIRE.

SOMETHING MY EMPLOYERS HAVE BEEN SEEKING FOR A HUNDRED YEARS.

...WHY DO YOU WANT TO KNOW ABOUT THAT?

YOU'RE ALREADY AT THE HEART OF IT.

YOU'RE ALREADY INVOLVED— SCRATCH THAT.

NEXT TIME, IT MIGHT NOT BE THE DUMMY— IT'LL BE YOUR OWN FACE THAT GETS BLOWN OFF.

DID YOU FORGET? WHETHER WE WANT IT OR NOT, THERE'S SOMEBODY WHO'S GOING TO SPREAD THE INFORMATION FOR US.

I'M SABARA-MOND!

HOW ARE WE SUPPOSED TO BE DECOYS?

PARADE AROUND THE CITY IN A FLOAT, ANNOUNCING, "I AM THE LEADER OF SABARA-MOND!" TO EVERYONE?

SOUNDS KINDA FUN.

SO WHAT DO YOU THINK ABOUT MAKING HIM A FRIEND INSTEAD?

THOUGH IF WE TRIED TO MAKE HIM INTO A PAWN, IT'D PROBABLY BACKFIRE.

EVERYONE IN THE ORGANIZATION IS PROBABLY COOKING UP A WAY TO PUT AN END TO HIM.

AH HA HA HA!

DON'T DO THIS TO ME!

AH HA!

D-DON'T!

HAFF!

HAFF!!

I'M GONNA REOPEN MY WOUNDS...

...PIPE DOWN.

AH HA HA HA HA HA HA!

HAAH, THAT WAS A GOOD LAUGH.

I FEEL BAD FOR HIM, SO I THINK I'LL FORGIVE HIM FOR ABANDONING ME.

SORRY, SORRY.

IT'S JUST TOO MUCH!

KOFF!

THIS MEANS HE'S GOTTEN BUDDY-BUDDY WITH SOLITAIRE, RIGHT? I WONDER IF I CAN GET HIS AUTOGRAPH.

BUT MAN, I ENVY HIGURO-SAN.

I HOPE SHE'S PLAYING NICE WITH THOSE KIDS.

AND MAJIRI...

THIS IS THE PLACE, RIGHT? WHERE SOLITAIRE MADE HIS APPEARANCE.

I HEAR THERE'S A PRETTY FAMOUS FORTUNE-TELLER IN THERE TOO.

SO THAT'S... THE BUILDING.

...I WONDER IF MY DEAR LITTLE KIDSASSIN-KUN IS IN.

WOULD YOU HAPPEN TO KNOW?

YOU HAVE EXCELLENT TIMING. I WAS JUST HOPING I'D HAVE THE CHANCE TO SAY HELLO.

YOU'RE WITH THE HEILEI... AREN'T YOU?

TA TA TA TA TA (TAPPA)

......

THAT BOY IS GOING TO BECOME MY LITTLE BROTHER, SO THAT MAKES US...SOON-TO-BE RELATIVES.

...IT CONCERNS XIAOYU-KUN.

PEKO (BOW)

SURU (SWF)

!

CALLING YOUR FRIENDS WHEN I'M—

DON'T BE RUDE.

KA (CLACK)

GICHI (YANK)

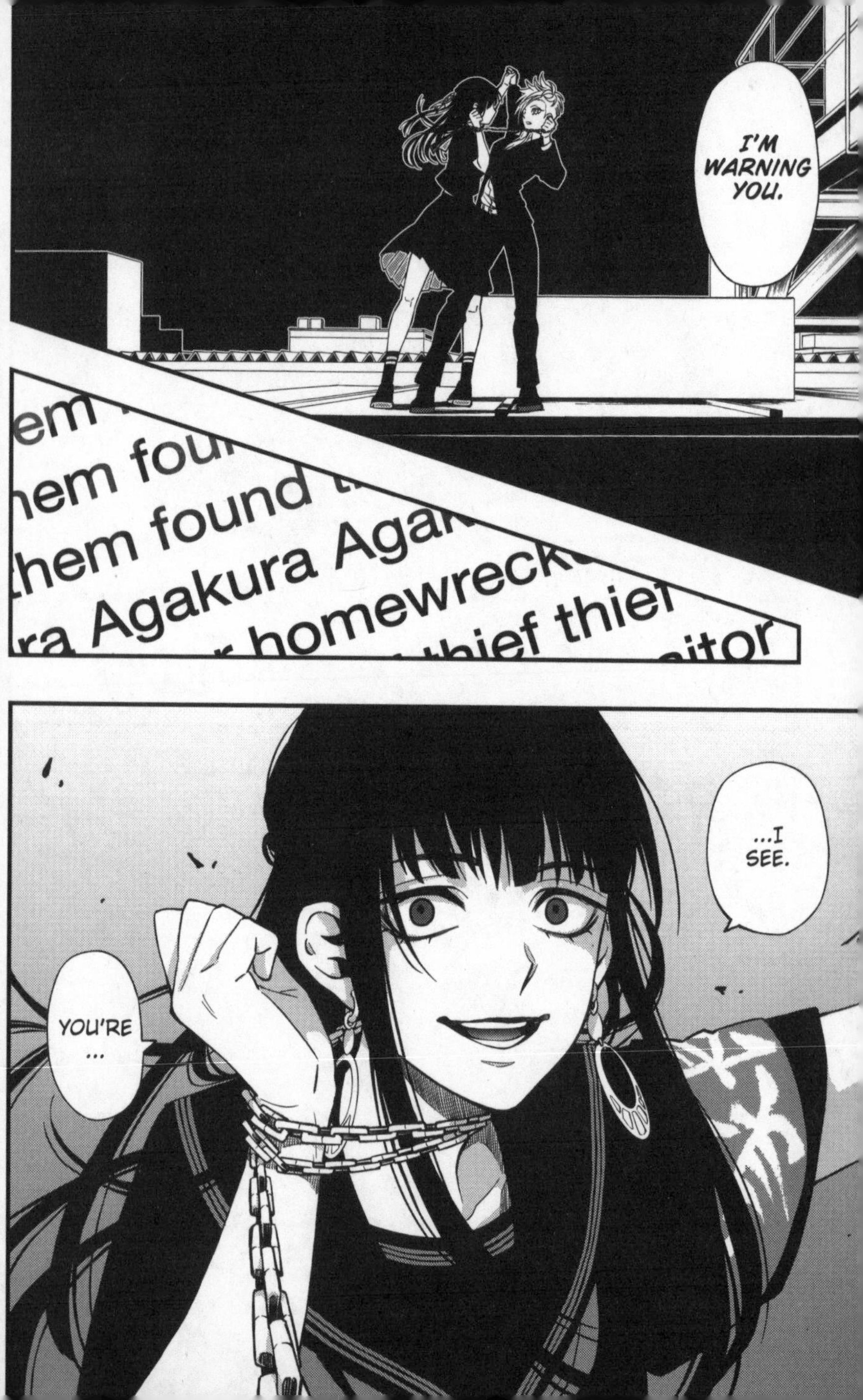
I'M WARNING YOU.
em
hem fou
them found
them found
ra Agakura Agak
homewreck
ra Agakura
thief thief
itor
...I SEE.
YOU'RE ...

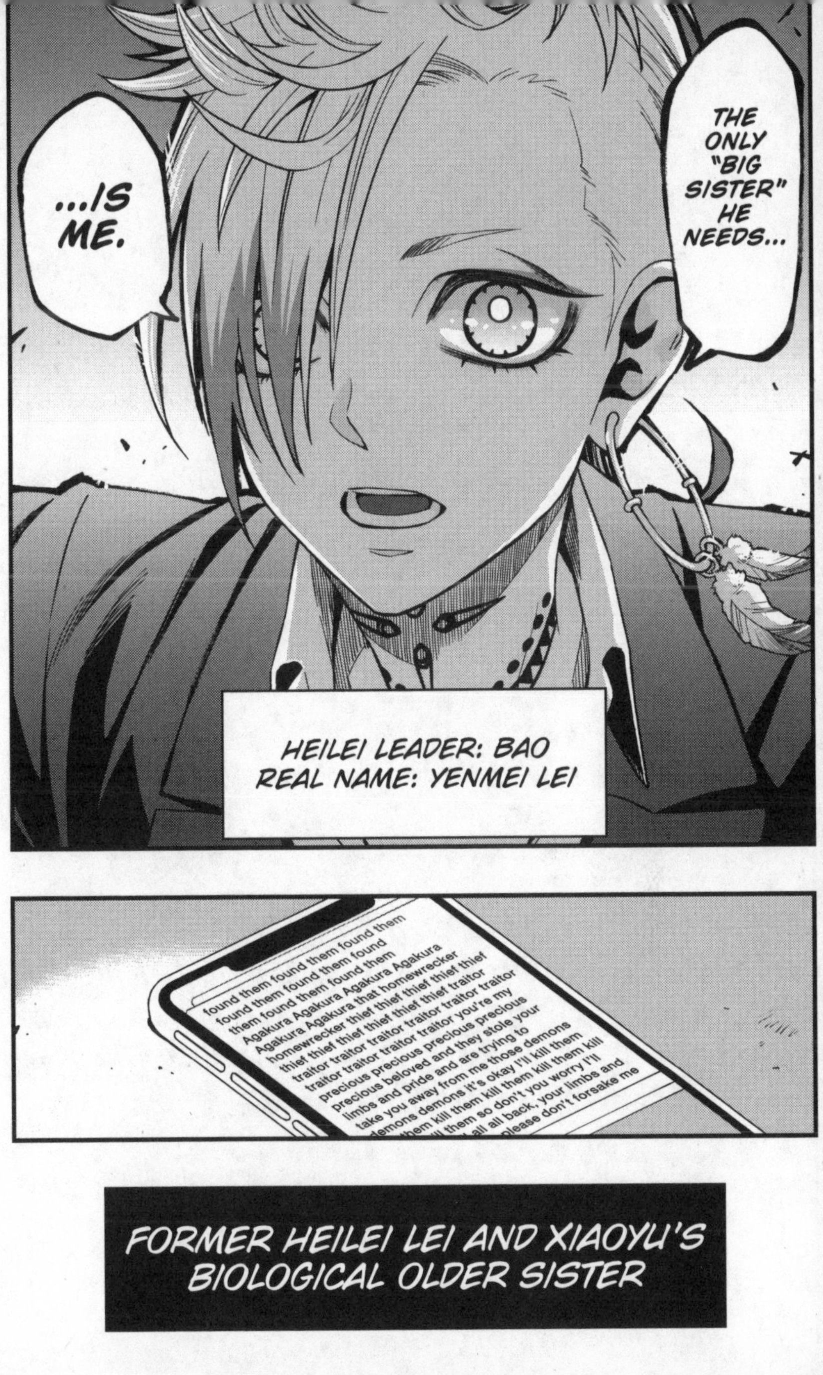
THE ONLY "BIG SISTER" HE NEEDS...
...IS ME.
HEILEI LEADER: BAO
REAL NAME: YENMEI LEI
found them found them found them
found them found them found
them found them found them
Agakura Agakura Agakura Agakura
Agakura Agakura that homewrecker
homewrecker thief thief thief thief
thief thief thief thief thief traitor
traitor traitor traitor traitor traitor
traitor traitor traitor traitor you're my
precious precious precious precious
precious beloved and they stole your
limbs and pride and are trying to
take you away from me those demons
demons demons it's okay I'll kill them
them kill them kill them kill them kill
them so don't you worry I'll
all all back, your limbs and
please don't forsake me
FORMER HEILEI LEI AND XIAOYU'S
BIOLOGICAL OLDER SISTER

DEAD MOUNT
DEATH PLAY

...THEN YOU SHOULDN'T HAVE ANY PROBLEM WITH ME BUYING HIM, RIGHT?

IF YOU DON'T CONSIDER HIM FAMILY AND HAVE WRITTEN HIM OFF AS A "BROKEN TOOL"...

I DON'T WANT TO HEAR ANY "I COULD NEVER SELL MY PRECIOUS SON" NOW, YOU HEAR?

#70

I'D LIKE TO HEAR EVERYONE'S OPINION.

THAT IS WHAT ROZAN-SAMA SAID, BUT...

...I WOULD REGRET LOSING A BODY THAT COULD SERVE AS THE FOUNDATION FOR A T'ING-FU.

IF ANY OF THIS WERE TO COME TO LIGHT, IT WOULD REFLECT POORLY ON OUR ALLIES, THE SHINOYAMA FAMILY.

CONSIDER THE ERA WE LIVE IN.

IF IT'S A MATTER OF RAW MATERIALS FOR T'ING-FU, COULDN'T WE SIMPLY ACQUIRE ANOTHER SUITABLE VESSEL FROM SOMEWHERE?

HA! THEN WE MIGHT AS WELL SELL HIM AT A HIGH PRICE.

WHICH IS WHY WE MUST KEEP IT SECRET WITHIN THE FAMILY.

IF YOU ASK ME, THE HEAD OF THE FAMILY IS BEING TOO INDULGENT SIMPLY BECAUSE THE BOY'S HIS BIOLOGICAL SON, DON'T YOU THINK?

...

THE HEILEI HAVE NO NEED FOR SOMEONE SO USELESS!

EVEN IF SHE WAS AN AGAKURA, THE ONE WHO LEFT HIM IN THAT STATE WAS A LITTLE GIRL!

IF YOU DON'T WANT TO MISS OUT ON A T'ING-FU, THEN JUST TELL OLD MAN SHINOYAMA THAT HE TOOK A TURN FOR THE WORSE AND DIED.

IN FACT, I'D HAPPILY DISPOSE OF HIM MY—

SHUN
(SWISH)

SELF.

...YOU DARE PLOT TO DECEIVE MASTER ROZAN?

!?

BOTO (GLOP)

WHAT INSOLENCE TOWARD MY FATHER, THE CURRENT HEAD OF THIS FAMILY.

AND...

ZASHU (SLASH)

...NGH!!!

DOSHA
(SPLAT)

...YOU HAVE INSULTED MY LITTLE BROTHER XIAOYU.

WHAT WAS THAT ABOUT THE HEILEI HAVING NO NEED FOR SOMEONE SO USELESS THAT EVEN A LITTLE GIRL COULD BEST THEM...?

I SEE...

MY DAUGHTER IS FIERCE.

WHEN I MENTIONED MAKING XIAOYU INTO A T'ING-FU...

...SHE EVEN TRIED TO KILL ME, HER FATHER.

OH, AM I MISTAKEN?

NOT QUITE.

SO THIS IS REVENGE... FOR THAT CUTE LITTLE KIDSASSIN-KUN.

I SEE...

YOU'RE RIGHT ABOUT CALLING XIAOYU "CUTE."

(TO LEAP)

グ いぃっ
(GUI (YANK))

THAT, WE CAN AGREE ON!

OH! YES!

I HATE YOU FOR MAIMING MY LITTLE BROTHER.

BUT I ALSO THANK YOU FOR IT.

グ
(GURU (WHIRL))

3

THAT'S UNEX-PECTED.

IT'S BECAUSE HE LOST HIS LIMBS...

...THAT HE WAS ABLE TO GET AWAY FROM THAT ACCURSED HOME.

GICHI (YANK)

THANK ME...YOU SAY?

BASA (FWAP)

JARA (JANGLE)

!?

NH! A DISTRAC-TION...!

I'M NOT INTERESTED IN ANTIQUATED VALUE SYSTEMS.

GASHA (KSHNK)

SARA

I THOUGHT THE HEILEI WERE MUCH MORE LOYAL TO THEIR FAMILY.

...IF YOU INTEND TO STEAL MY LITTLE BROTHER AWAY FROM ME, THEN...

HYUN (WHIRL)

I CONSIDERED IT, BUT...

THEN CAN I PERSUADE YOU TO TAKE IT EASY ON ME?

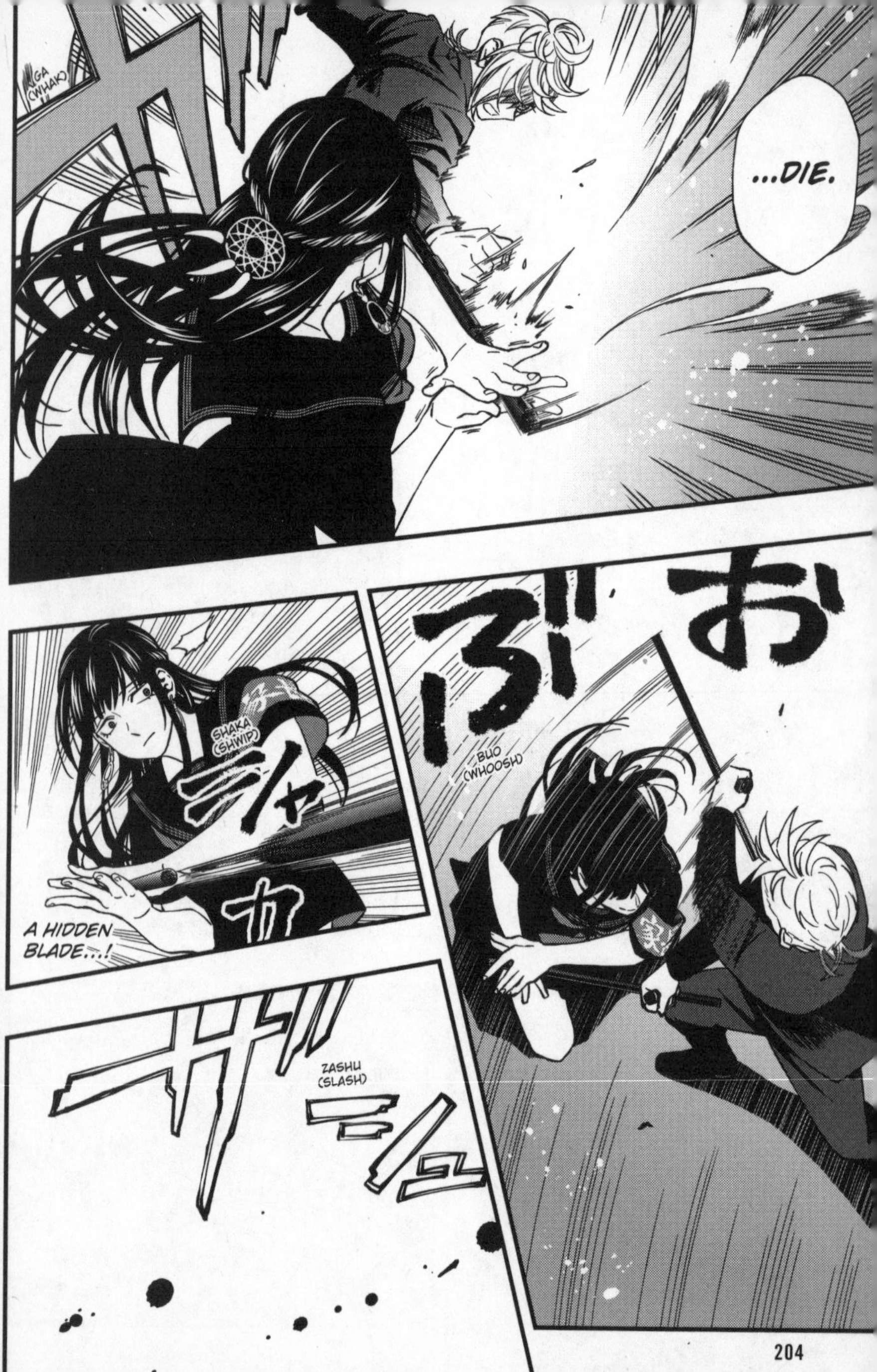
...DIE.
GA (WHAK)
ぶお
BUO (WHOOSH)
SHAKA (SHWIP)
シャカ
A HIDDEN BLADE...!
ZASHU (SLASH)
ザシュ

ARE THESE REALLY A SOURCE OF MAGICAL POWER?

WHERE I'M FROM, THEY COULD BE BOUGHT FOR MUCH LESS.

SO JEWELS ARE MY FUEL...

ISN'T THAT AWFULLY PRICEY?

IF YOU TOUCH IT, YOU'LL AUTOMATICALLY ABSORB ITS MAGIC AND BREAK THE STONE, SO BE CAREFUL.

YES. THEY SHOULD REPLENISH THE STRENGTH OF YOUR ARMS TOO.

SIGN: PAWN SHOP / WE BUY HIGH!

IT'S A FAR BETTER DEAL TO ONLY HAVE TO PAY MONEY FOR IT.

BESIDES, CASTING SOME SPELLS REQUIRES YOUR MEMORY, LIFE, OR SACRIFICING A BODY PART...

THE MORE TRANSPARENT AND LARGER IT IS, THE MORE MAGIC IS IN IT.

SO THAT'S WHY MISTRESS SAYO WAS ACCUMULATING SO MANY JEWELS...

IF RAW ORE WILL WORK, YOU COULD BUY MORE OF IT CHEAPER, YOU KNOW?

I SEE... IT'S NOT LIKE YOU COULD GO WALKING AROUND WITH A TON OF RAW ORE ON YOU ANYWAY...

BASICALLY, DOUBLING THE WEIGHT OF A JEWEL INCREASES ITS MAGIC POWER TENFOLD...

IT'S EXPONENTIAL, NOT SIMPLY ADDITIVE.

I CAN'T TURN TO ROZAN-SAN FOR A NUMBER OF REASONS...

SO NOW THE ONLY ISSUE IS THE MATTER OF MONEY.

...IF HIS VESSEL WAS BURNED OR CHOPPED UP, CHANCES ARE IT WOULD AFFECT HIS SOUL AS WELL.

I CAN ONLY ASCERTAIN HIS SPIRITUAL SAFETY, BUT...

DO YOU THINK THE REAL POLKA-KUN IS STILL ALL RIGHT...?

EEEK!

BO (BLAZE)

GUARDING MISTRESS SAYO AND POLKA WAS MY DUTY.

DON'T SAY THAT—

THIS IS ALL MY FAULT...

I WAS THE ONLY ONE OF THE GUARDS WHO KNEW THAT STUFFED ANIMAL WAS THE REAL POLKA.

THAT'S WHY I BEAR THE RESPONSI-BILITY.

YOU'RE JUST GOING TO BLURT IT RIGHT OUT?

"THE STUFFED ANIMAL HOUSING YOUR SON'S SOUL HAS BEEN KIDNAPPED"?

...IN ANY CASE, WE HAVE TO REPORT THIS TO ROZAN-SAN...

...

OH! RIGHT... TODAY'S...

HUH?

IT'S IMPOS-SIBLE.

WE CAN'T NOT TELL HIM.

MY GRANDFATHER'S SUPPOSED TO GO TO THE HOSPITAL FOR A CHECKUP THIS AFTERNOON.

IT'S JUST A ROUTINE VISIT, BUT...

...DEPENDING ON WHAT THEY FIND, THEY MIGHT WANT TO DO A LAPAROSCOPY ON HIM, WHICH MEANS HE'LL BE UNDER GENERAL ANESTHESIA AND IN NO CONDITION FOR A CONVERSATION.

HUH?

I'M THE WORST.

WELL...YOU'D PROBABLY BE ADMITTED TO THE HOSPITAL TOO.

AND IF YOU WERE TO TRY AND TELL ANYONE ELSE IN THE FAMILY THAT POLKA'S BEEN PUT IN A STUFFED SHARK THAT GOT KIDNAPPED...

I THOUGHT IT WOULD GIVE ME THE CHANCE TO GET POLKA BACK SAFELY BEFORE MASTER FOUND OUT ABOUT MY BLUNDER.

EVEN THOUGH IT WAS ONLY FOR A MOMENT... I WAS ALMOST RELIEVED.

THAT YOU FEEL THAT WAY JUST GOES TO SHOW YOU'RE A DECENT PERSON.

IT CAN'T BE HELPED.

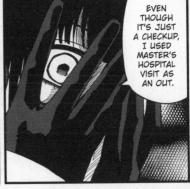

EVEN THOUGH IT'S JUST A CHECKUP, I USED MASTER'S HOSPITAL VISIT AS AN OUT.

AFTER ALL, I'M...

I DON'T DESERVE THAT PRAISE.

THOUGH MOST WERE FOUND OUT AND KILLED FOR IT.

FRAUDULENT ACCOUNTING! GRAFTERS SHOULD BE PUT TO DEATH!

FALSE REPORT!

IMPERIAL GORGEOUS UNIT, VICE CAPTAIN OF THE ASSESSMENT BUREAU

JANGRAD DIMORIGH XIV

IN THE EMPIRE, THERE WERE PLENTY OF PEOPLE WHO WOULD LAYER LIES UPON LIES IN THEIR REPORTS.

THAT'S NONE OF YOUR—

CAN YOU REALLY SAY IT'S NONE OF MY BUSINESS GIVEN THE SITUATION?

!!

DO YOU RESENT HAVING TO PROTECT THE REAL POLKA-KUN?

LET'S HAVE A LITTLE TALK.

WE CAN TAKE IT SLOW.

....!

HOW RECENTLY?

BUT IN ALL HONESTY...IT'S ONLY RECENTLY THAT I'VE REALIZED I HATE HIM DEEP DOWN.

...THERE'S SOMETHING ABOUT HIM...I'VE NEVER LIKED.

THAT HE COULD SUGGEST THAT, WITHOUT ANY REGARD FOR MASTER'S FEELINGS...

WHEN YOU REVEALED THAT SHARK'S TRUE IDENTITY WAS POLKA.

...AND NOW THE SPOILED BOY SAYS HE'D RATHER HAVE A ROBOT BODY THAN GET HIS ORIGINAL BODY BACK.

I CARRY THESE ARMS AND LEGS I RECEIVED FROM ROZAN-SAMA WITH PRIDE.

IT'S NOT LIKE I'D WANT HIM TO LET ME TAKE HIS PLACE INSTEAD.

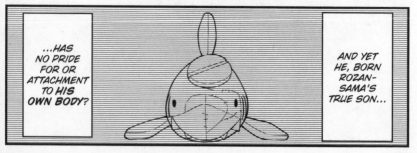

...HAS NO PRIDE FOR OR ATTACHMENT TO HIS OWN BODY?

AND YET HE, BORN ROZAN-SAMA'S TRUE SON...

EVEN NOW, I WISH TO SUPPORT ROZAN-SAMA LIKE A REAL SON.

I'VE ALWAYS WANTED TO BE ROZAN-SAMA'S CHILD.

I WANTED TO LUNGE AT HIM THAT VERY MOMENT...

I CAN NEVER BE HIS REAL SON.

AND YET... WE'LL NEVER HAVE ANY BIOLOGICAL CONNECTION.

GU
(GRIT)

STILL... THAT BRAT... TAKES WHAT HE HAS FOR GRANTED...

FORGET IT.

I'M JUST JEALOUS OF HIM, PURE AND SIMPLE.

NEVER MIND... THAT'S ALL EXCUSES.

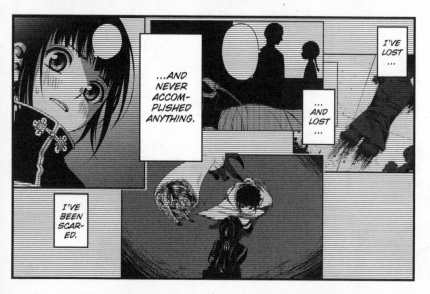

...AND NEVER ACCOMPLISHED ANYTHING.

I'VE LOST...

...AND LOST...

I'VE BEEN SCARED.

IT WAS SOMETHING I YEARNED FOR.

...WAS SOMETHING THAT WILL NEVER BE COMPROMISED BY THOSE THINGS.

WHAT WAS PARADED BEFORE MY EYES...

I'M SO... PATHETIC...

EVEN THE THRONE WAS AN INHERITED POSITION.

IN MY COUNTRY... BLOOD RELATIONS WERE VALUED.

BUT MY BIOLOGICAL FATHER...

THAT'S WHY I ALSO ENVY THE BONDS WITHIN FAMILIES THAT SHARE THE SAME BLOOD.

...!

AND IN THE END, HE STABBED ME FOR HIS OWN GREED.

...SOLD ME FOR MONEY.

DOSU (SHUNK)

AND I FIRMLY BELIEVE THAT FEELING GOES BOTH WAYS.

...AS IF ROZAN-SAN WERE FAMILY.

BUT I KNOW THAT YOU FEEL JUST AS BONDED...

I'M SURE THAT, BLOOD ASIDE, YOUR SOULS ARE BOUND.

SO THAT CONNEC- TION...

...SHOULD BE TREA- SURED AS WELL.

...WOULD HURT JUST AS DEEPLY.

BECAUSE THE PAIN IF IT WAS SEVERED...

THAT'S WHY... THIS TIME FOR SURE...

...I MUST WORK TO BUILD A WORLD WHERE EVERYONE CAN LIVE PEACEFULLY TOGETHER...

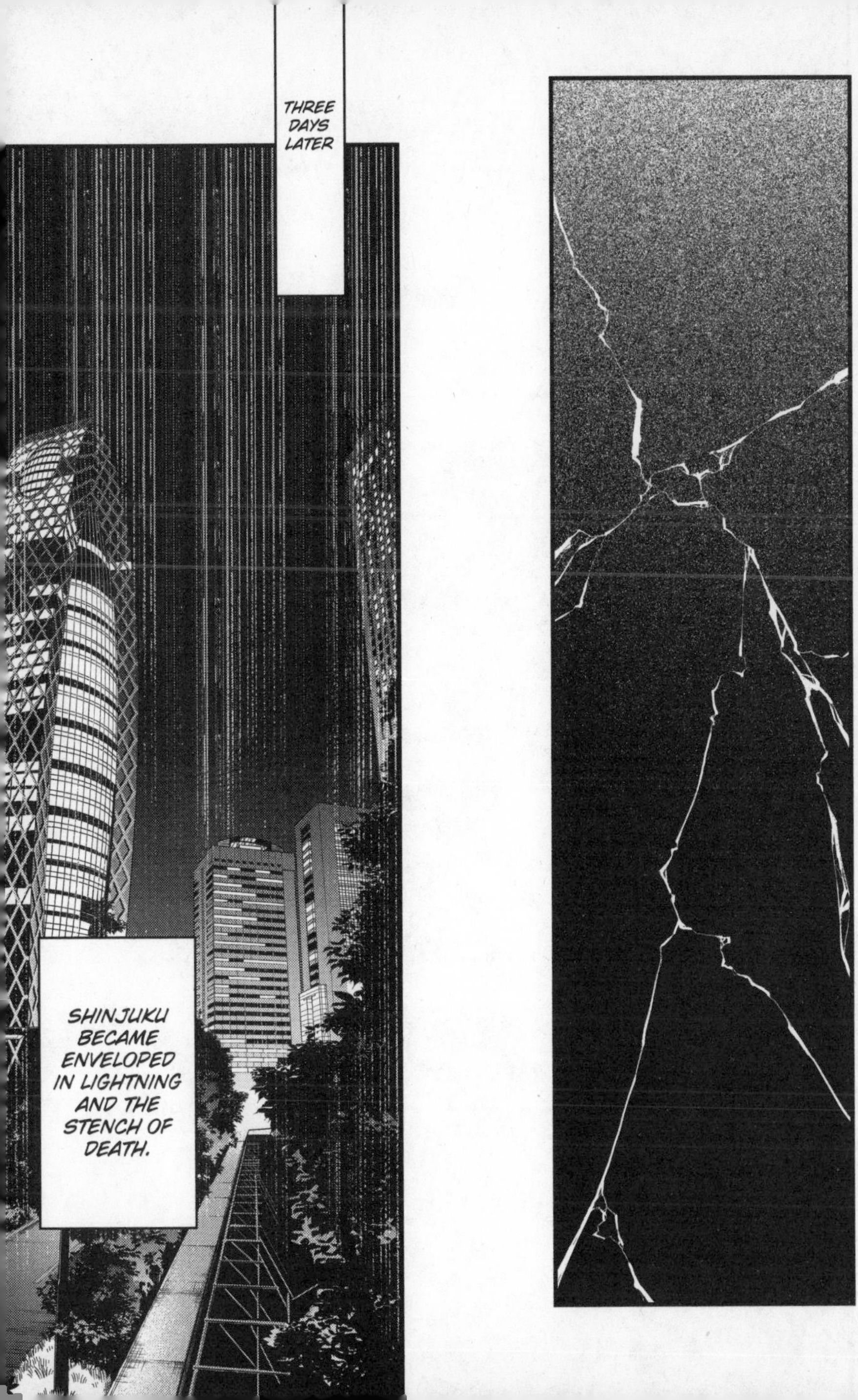
THREE DAYS LATER
SHINJUKU BECAME ENVELOPED IN LIGHTNING AND THE STENCH OF DEATH.

NOW...

...LET'S TURN THE WORLD INSIDE OUT.

"CORPSE GOD."

YOU ACHIEVED AS MUCH ONCE BEFORE.

DEAD MOUNT DEATH PLAY 8 END

SPECIAL. THANKS

WRITER:
RYOHGO NARITA

EDITOR:
KAZUHIDE SHIMIZU

TRANSLATION HELP:
JUYOUN LEE (YEN PRESS)

MAGIC RESEARCH:
KIYOMUNE MIWA
(TEAM BARREL ROLL)

STAFF:
YOSHICHIKA EGUCHI
YOSHIE_Y.UNO
OTO
NANAMI HASAMA
NORA

TRANSLATION NOTES

COMMON HONORIFICS

no honorific: Indicates familiarity or closeness; if used without permission or reason, addressing someone in this manner would constitute an insult.

-san: The Japanese equivalent of Mr./Mrs./Miss. If a situation calls for politeness, this is the fail-safe honorific.

-sama: Conveys great respect; may also indicate the social status of the speaker is lower than that of the addressee.

-kun: Used most often when referring to boys, this indicates affection or familiarity. Occasionally used by older men among their peers, but it may also be used by anyone referring to a person of lower standing.

-chan: An affectionate honorific indicating familiarity used mostly in reference to girls; also used in reference to cute persons or animals of either gender.

-senpai: A suffix used to address upperclassmen or more experienced coworkers.

-sensei: A respectful term for teachers, artists, or high-level professionals.

[o]nee: Japanese equivalent to "older sis."
[o]nii: Japanese equivalent to "older bro."

CURRENCY CONVERSION

While exchange rates fluctuate daily, a good approximation is ¥100 to 1 USD.

Page 100

Sunkei and *hakkei* both refer to a Chinese style of martial arts known as *fa jin* that involves imbuing massive explosive energy into a strike at the very last second. It's sometimes called the "one-inch punch" in English.

Page 184

Solitaire's stage name is made up of characters from his real name, Sorimura Tena.

DEAD MOUNT
DEATH PLAY

Super-Fun Illustrated Guide to
DEAD MOUNT DEATH PLAY

SPECIMEN

SOLITAIRE TV

Chat ∨

- It's heeeeere!!
- It's here!
- Welcome back!
- we've been waiting
- welcome home, you funny old man
- it's here
- can't wait
- Please leave...
- you kidding me?
- wonder how long before this one gets taken down...

HIDE CHAT REPLAY

A transient channel that will suddenly appear and just as suddenly vanish when it gets reported. Even so, Solitaire's hard-core fans have saved all the videos he's ever put up. He mainly uploads videos of his activities as a criminal for pleasure, but many of his videos feature him traveling to haunted locations in search of paranormal phenomena.

As it happens, Solitaire's most-viewed video has nothing to do with his crimes or paranormal phenomena. The video shows him demonstrating harmless magic tricks to a litter of kittens and their awed little faces.

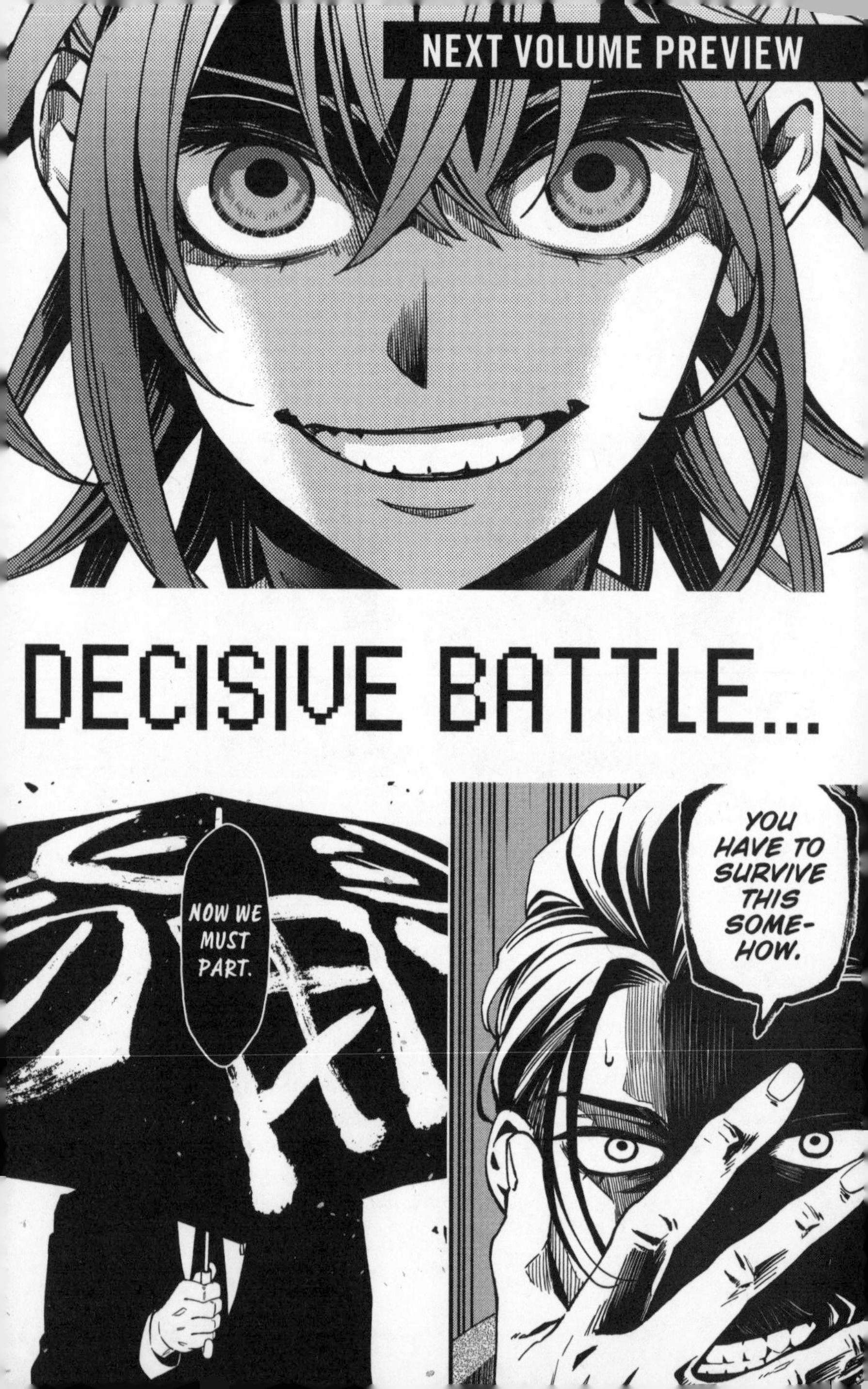
NEXT VOLUME PREVIEW
DECISIVE BATTLE...
YOU HAVE TO SURVIVE THIS SOME-HOW.
NOW WE MUST PART.

DEAD MOUNT DEATH PLAY

Before Civil and Polka launch into battle, a look into the past reveals the connection between Civil and Fire-breathing Bug, the end result of those burdened with the blame. As past collides with present, the revelation of "Corpse God's" true name brings further unexpected truths to light. Filled with conflicting thoughts and perceptions, the intense conflict begins...

LOOK OUT FOR THE

TO BE CONTINUED.........

DEAD MOUNT DEATH PLAY

8

STORY: **Ryohgo Narita**   ART: **Shinta Fujimoto**

Translation: Christine Dashiell * Lettering: Abigail Blackman

DEAD MOUNT DEATH PLAY Volume 8 ©2021 Ryohgo Narita, Shinta Fujimoto/SQUARE ENIX CO., LTD. First published in Japan in 2021 by SQUARE ENIX CO., LTD. English translation rights arranged with SQUARE ENIX CO., LTD. and Yen Press, LLC through Tuttle-Mori Agency, Inc., Tokyo.

English translation ©2022 by SQUARE ENIX CO., LTD.

Yen Press • 150 West 30th Street, 19th Floor • New York, NY 10001

Visit us at yenpress.com
facebook.com/yenpress
twitter.com/yenpress
yenpress.tumblr.com
instagram.com/yenpress

First Yen Press Edition: September 2022
The chapters in this volume were originally published as ebooks by Yen Press.
Edited by Abigail Blackman and Yen Press Editorial: Won Young Seo, Kurt Hassler
Designed by Yen Press Design: Lilliana Checo, Wendy Chan

Yen Press is an imprint of Yen Press, LLC.
The Yen Press name and logo are trademarks of Yen Press, LLC.

The publisher is not responsible for websites (or their content) that are not owned by the publisher.

Library of Congress Control Number: 2018953479

ISBNs: 978-1-9753-4958-5 (paperback)
          978-1-9753-4959-2 (ebook)

10 9 8 7 6 5 4 3 2 1

WOR

Printed in the United States of America

Turn to the back of the book to read an exclusive bonus short story by Ryohgo Narita!

DEAD MOUNT DEATH PLAY

Episode **8**:
Barrier of Coursing Blood

VOLUMES 1-16 IN STORES NOW!

VOLUMES 1-17 AVAILABLE DIGITALLY!

Toilet-bound Hanako-Kun

At Kamome Academy, rumors abound about the school's Seven Mysteries, one of which is Hanako-san. Said to occupy the third stall of the third floor girls' bathroom in the old school building, Hanako-san grants any wish when summoned. Nene Yashiro, an occult-loving high school girl who dreams of romance, ventures into this haunted bathroom...but the Hanako-san she meets there is nothing like she imagined! Kamome Academy's Hanako-san...is a boy!

Yen Press

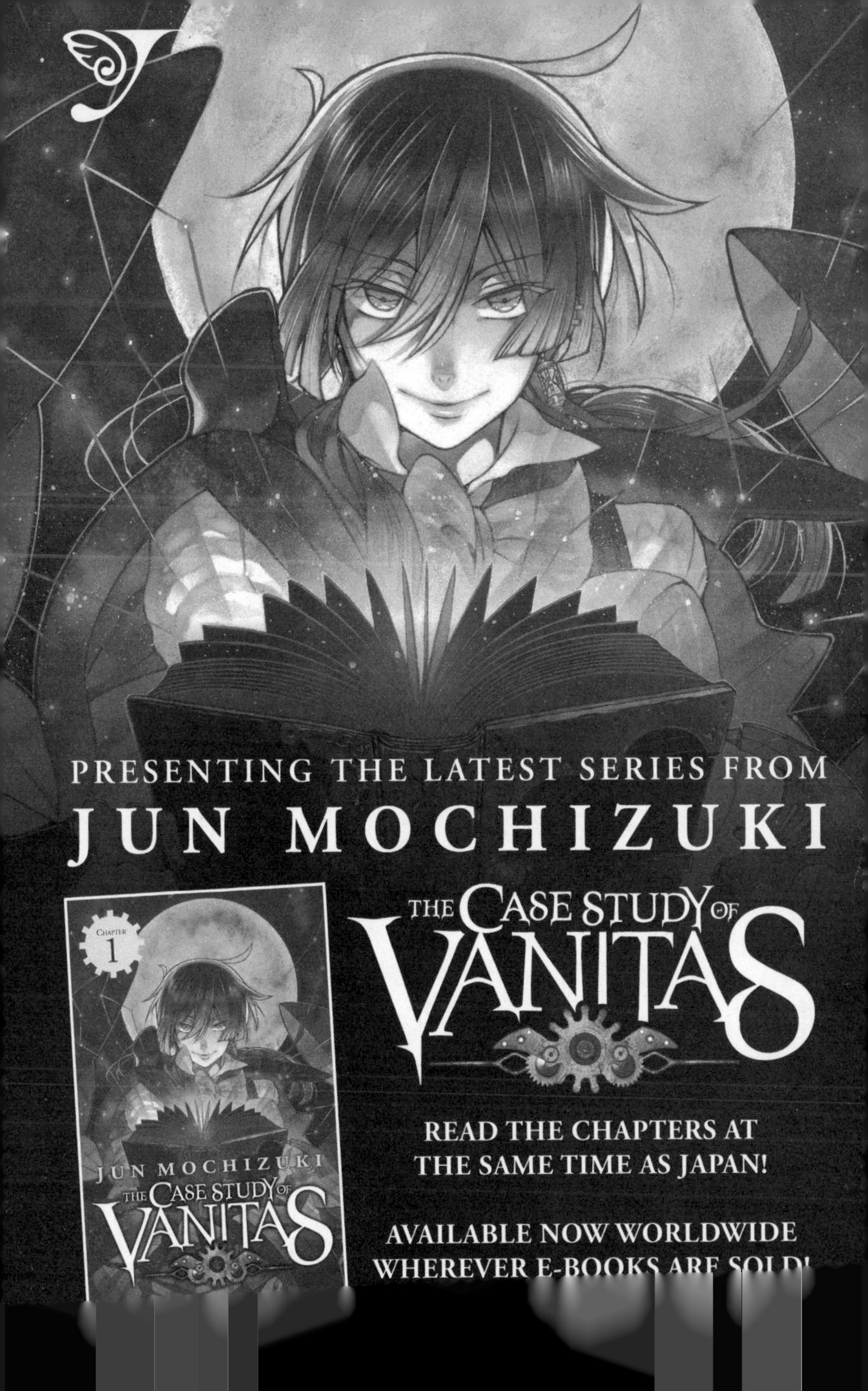
PRESENTING THE LATEST SERIES FROM
JUN MOCHIZUKI
THE CASE STUDY OF VANITAS
READ THE CHAPTERS AT
THE SAME TIME AS JAPAN!
AVAILABLE NOW WORLDWIDE
WHEREVER E-BOOKS ARE SOLD!
CHAPTER 1
JUN MOCHIZUKI
THE CASE STUDY OF VANITAS

DEAD MOUNT
DEATH PLAY

That wasn't to say that person had disappeared. Silk determined that the attacker had been invisible from the very start, and she muttered as a dark irritation came over her face. "……I see. They knew that the farce would never work on me……so they only used me as a decoy."

"What on earth……?!"

"It's possible that it was 'The Alchemy Scholar' Pani's duds…… One of 'Clear Bright Doll' Medeon's copies."

As though in response to Silk's mutterings, a faint lightning crackle flickered at Izliz's back; Shagrua could sense only that something humanoid was there. However, he couldn't detect any magic power or life force. His only guess was that an invisible entity had acted on its own to stab Izliz.

Shagrua wanted to run to Izliz to help her, but the pipe she held shook, and from beneath her bone mask came a great plume of smoke. At the sight of it, he stopped.

Acting for all the world as though nothing were amiss, Izliz grasped the invisible stake protruding from her chest.

"I can't believe Pani's rejected hunk of junk was tamed by Geldwood."

Then, very slowly, she turned around…and an evil laugh seeped out from beneath her mask as she growled, "I'm no vampire, yet you thought a stake to the heart would be enough to kill me?"

Her words dripped with ironic sarcasm, but Shagrua's Evil Eye detected another phenomenon aside from Medeon. It was still far off, but an immense soul energy—a veritable torrent of distorted life—was on its way.

The Church's protégé, Dragon…

Oh boy…… It looks like that rotten saint really wants to crush us.

"……Fine by me."

Conjuring up magic power within her body, Izliz spat out those words with all the indifference in the world.

"If it's a fight you want…then I accept."

was suggesting he accept death and surrender himself to Izliz. If Silk took only some of his blood, Izliz's necromancy could preserve his body, and later, a skilled holy practitioner might resurrect him.

It's true that with her powers......I should be able to fake my death. She might have her own reasons for saddling herself with the burden of being an enemy of the world.

Filled with thoughts that never would have crossed his mind had he not fought the Corpse God and read the diary he had left behind, Shagrua continued wordlessly swinging his blade. Silk was still far from trying her hardest here. He had to weigh his options and make a decision now. A decision about what action he would take and, depending on the situation, whether he was ready to die first to achieve it.

But, for starters......   Will Madam Izliz agree to resurrect me?

"Good grief, you so easily assume you get to work a person to the bone whenever it pleases you, don't you? You really were raised an aristocrat," Izliz complained sardonically while waving her pipe. It still looked like she was trying her hardest to keep the building intact, but these lesser attacks wouldn't kill Shagrua. Izliz had calculated that if Silk intended to skewer Shagrua's magic-fortified body, it would take a level of attack high enough to bring down a castle wall. "......But why would the goons at Geldwood send Crimson Snow here at this particular point in time?"

She devoted some thought to the current situation. "The only thing I can think of is—"

She never finished her last words, because just then, Izliz's heart was stabbed through her back.

"?!"

Shagrua and Silk both stopped dead at the sight.

"Madam Izliz?!"

"That's......" Silk narrowed her eyes as she grasped the situation. From the very place where Izliz's heart should be protruded something that looked like a stake dyed the color of blood, but there was no sign of whomever had delivered the fatal skewering.

Corpse God's spirit had possessed Shagrua.

For some reason, they've deemed Shagrua an obstacle and want him gone......

Having spoken to the man herself, she knew there was no mistaking the Church's intent.

However, she could not so easily break her contract. This was because the reward her client promised was of considerable importance to her.

She recalled the words the holy priest-client had said to her:

"What we can offer you, a creature we would not usually associate with, is information.

"It pertains to your little sister 'Godhead Restorer' Madam Riddhe......

"We have information that about one hundred years ago, she traveled from here to a certain other world.

"We shall supply you with the means to travel to that world......Terra Mater."

"I see. I see clearly now that you are a virtuous man."

"That's...giving me too much credit," Shagrua said, casting his eyes downward in a gesture suggesting he truly didn't believe in his own virtue.

At the same moment, one of the icicles flew at him without making a sound. But though his eyes were turned down, Shagrua hadn't stopped paying attention. Detecting the faint magic power encasing the icicle, he sliced it out of the air with one sweep of his sword.

As though she had predicted this course of action, the red icicles came two, then three, and finally four at a time, their numbers steadily growing until, at last, it was as if a swarm of locusts with its own sense of direction attacked Shagrua.

He parried them all.

"As I have been commissioned, I mean to kill you. However, that is as far as my job goes."

"......?"

"I will take some of your blood, but what happens after I have completed my work is none of my concern," Silk said, flicking her eyes toward Izliz.

That was enough for Shagrua to understand his opponent's intention. The Church's technology for detecting the location of a soul. To escape that, she

head, prompting the red icicles floating around them to rotate to match her movement.

"I knew that already, but......is this some kind of standard of etiquette among the knights of the church?"

"If you were to kill the wrong person, it would put a stain on your reputation of only killing those who are your targets. So there's no need to sound me out like earlier. I truly am Shagrua, so promise me you won't get anyone else involved."

Sound him out......he says? I'd planned on ending this with my first move, Silk grumbled in her head as she watched her opponent.

A little ways off, she saw Izliz's shoulders trembling. Something about Shagrua was not as she'd expected, so she was undoubtedly perplexed by his direct delivery. Silk returned her gaze to Shagrua and continued to ponder him as she studied him.

Why should he be concerned about my reputation......? What an odd man. He's not quite how he was described in the information I received, but......he doesn't strike me as a bad man.

Her client had asked that she "dispose of Shagrua, whose body has been possessed by the Corpse God," but she'd been able to tell that was a lie from the moment she laid eyes on her target.

This man is not the Corpse God.

Silk was no possessor of an Evil Eye, but having excelled at observing others' life forces as a vampire, she could discern in a moment whether he had been possessed by that necromancer's spirit.

I've been tricked, Silk thought. The client who had commissioned this job was from the highest echelons of the Geldwood Church, one of the holy priests.

They'd said they wanted her to release Shagrua's flesh from this evil curse and avenge those who had been killed by the Corpse God, but lies could only go so far.

There were records of the Corpse God having attacked the soldiers of the Church one hundred years ago, but there were no records of him having actively killed anyone in recent years. In fact, even in the decisive battle against "Calamity Crusher" Shagrua, the genius hieromancer Recuria, who could resurrect someone even from just a severed torso, had been serving right by his side. Silk couldn't imagine Recuria would miss the fact that the

over which he had no control. In a sense, most of Shagrua's battles were against enemies who far outranked him.

He'd been able to take the upper hand in his fight against the Wood Mage Romelka, but this was only due to the fact that she had had little to no intention of actually killing him. And with Izliz, it had been hard to devise a winning strategy even when he had been fully prepared from the start to challenge her.

No matter how those around him elevated him, he was no legendary hero— and he knew it. That's why he tried to learn as much about his opponent as he could to find any way he might win, no matter what unrefined method that required.

"......Madam Izliz is right. I have no intention of destroying the town. Why don't we go elsewhere?" Having nothing to lose, Shagrua offered the assassin this proposal.

Silk looked uncertain about accepting it.

Ordinarily, an assassin had no need to hear what her prey had to say, but on this occasion, Shagrua and Silk weren't alone. Izliz, who had herself asked them to take their fight somewhere else, was still present, and chances were good that Silk would obey Izliz's request in order to avoid a confrontation with an enemy so obviously powerful.

"......" Silk gave no reply, but she slid her gaze toward Izliz for a brief moment.

Shagrua was sure that with just one more prod, she would agree.

But the next moment, Shagrua found himself saying something that had nothing to do with their negotiation.

"Oh, that reminds me. I have another request first."

"......What is it? I don't make it a particular habit to converse with my targets."

"I still haven't told you my name."

"......Come again?" For a moment, the gloomy air about her wavered, and in the shadow of the cloak concealing her head, Silk furrowed her brow.

Shagrua paid no mind to the change and barreled onward, adhering to his own protocol before any battle by introducing himself.

"My name is Shagrua Edith Lugrid."

"......???"

Silk was utterly perplexed, and after a lengthy pause, she cocked her

nations, as she would sometimes cause mayhem in order to accomplish her brazen assassinations of even the most powerful political figures. A vampire noble touted as an enemy of the world but at the same time revered as a hero by a faction of the people.

Facing her for the first time, Shagrua studied his opponent.

Gloomy.

That was his first impression. If pressed to comment based on outside appearances alone, he would describe her as a woman with a somewhat dark air about her. However, she had a dignified bearing, and there was certainly nothing coarse in her demeanor. Instead, Shagrua felt all too keenly that she must be an aristocrat of some country.

Yet he could not shake that impression of gloom about her.

It seemed to come from the heaviness of the air he could feel enshrouding her. The weight of it didn't seem to be directed against him, her adversary. Rather, it felt as if she herself were being crushed by its weight. Here, in the midst of this scene, surrounded by hundreds of thousands of red icicles, where a certain kind of glamor hung in the air, it was as though he could see a heaviness of the air around her dragging everything down into a dark pit. Even setting aside the situation, Shagrua did not suppose that any rival emitting such a crushing pressure could ever be considered any ordinary person.

From what he'd found in texts in the Geldwood Church, he had a grasp—to a certain degree—of her combat capabilities. However, confronted with her in this moment, he understood that this was an enemy who was levels higher than anything he had even imagined. Depending on the circumstances, Shagrua imagined she might rival even Corpse God, but given her completely different temperament, it was pointless to even compare the two. The very notion was a distraction from clear thought, and he dismissed the comparison from his mind and refocused.

He still wanted to get out as much information about his opponent as possible, even if she was basically something straight out of a fairy tale.

After all, that was the only kind of opponent that Shagrua, who was called "Calamity Crusher," had ever taken on. What's more, he himself was no hero from a fairy tale, so he had no choice but to continue to walk in a reality

"......I know your name very well," Shagrua said, responding to his opponent's introduction while carefully picking and choosing from the wealth of information in his head.

The elder sister's name was "Crimson Snow" Silk Malacougar.
The younger sister's name was "Godhead Restorer" Riddhe Malacougar.

The sisters had not been seen in recent years and were perceived as something straight out of legend, or perhaps characters from a fairy tale. Even Shagrua had thought of them as such. However, he had to admit that this was no fairy tale he was now facing. One of the sisters, the elder Silk, stood directly in front of him, the target of her assassination attempt.

So......this is Crimson Snow.

"Crimson Snow" Silk had made a name for herself throughout the land as an assassin and was known even among the general public.

In those continents where she was unknown or in other worlds, people would probably cock their heads and wonder, "How can someone who's an active assassin be so notorious?" A fair question, but there was one good reason to account for this: Before carrying out a job, Silk always notified the public first.

She would not alert the target directly, but on the notice boards outside taverns and other conspicuous locations in the town where the target lived, as well as on the walls of churches and castles, she would declare her name and lethal intentions in red blood.

It goes without saying that the individual, thus warned of her intentions, would do all they could to strengthen their personal protection, but in the end, they always wound up robbed of all their blood, drained down to the last drop so that even resurrection sorcery could not work on them.

It really was a very vampiric way to kill. The majority of her victims were aristocrats and dishonest merchants who engaged in criminal cover-ups, executive members of criminal organizations, or heinous villains on the run. Although the more law-abiding the countries were critical of her actions, more often than not, the masses who had been tormented by the deceased praised and revered Silk as their savior.

Even so, she was decidedly regarded as an enemy of the world by most

and, in actuality, they can go about in broad daylight just fine.

They say that a vampire will die if stabbed in the heart with a special stake but that there are still some who can recover from such an attack.

They say that the Jester Dragon Norda waved this rumor off with a "Yeah, right. If there's a creature that won't die after taking a stake in the heart, then show 'em to me!"

They say that the Home-wrecker Dragon Malfy then brought "Wandering Balcony" Izliz before Norda.

They say that Wandering Balcony told Norda, "What kind of joke is that, you incompetent dragon?" and a fight broke out.

They say that the one who stopped the fight was the fifth rank among the Imperial Court Sorcerers of the Byandy Empire, a vampire youth.

They say that, in short, a fully developed vampire is incredibly strong and would be able to single-handedly hold their own against an entire army or even a dragon.

All manner of legends are told about vampires, but when it comes to their abilities, barely any are capable of exercising the full range of their potential. Put another way, one could say that as diverse and far-reaching as those powers may be, only a small fraction of vampires possess truly powerful abilities.

Vampires have always been few in number but among them are those who surpass full maturity and therefore possess even greater powers.

For example, Myrcadia Lulula who rules the principality of Djadjamnyl.

Her husband, Gardener Panan, who had instructed the Byandy Empire's "Roaming Woodlands" and was also a Wood Mage himself.

The fifth rank among the Imperial Court Sorcerers, "Scorching Nightwalker" Lake Bardish, who was active at the time of the empire's collapse.

Though they were few, the three vampires comprised the mercenary group Rot, which could upset the balance on any battlefield.

And then there were the sister vampires more famous than any other on the continent. Even now, 120 years since the duo were first defined as "enemies of the world," there has been no news of the pair ever having ever been defeated.

■ ■ ■

to the great knowledge they were able to amass through their impressive strength and long life spans, it was not uncommon for vampires to hold positions of power.

Unlike the long-lived peoples such as "The Alchemy Scholar" Pani and the Elemental Eye races, a vampire's vital functions slowed down as they aged, making their constitution more akin to the undead. Because of this, people described them as "alive while dead and dead while alive."

Due to their peculiar penchant for drinking others' blood, vampires had long been treated as monsters in many lands, but about five hundred years ago, a nation with a vampire as its ruler built up strength enough to cause a shift in the power balance.

Over time, vampires became more accepted by many countries on the continent. Perhaps due to vampires' small numbers, the vast majority of people have never seen one, and they are spoken of in an almost fairy tale-like way.

They say the first vampires were born as a result of relations between a dragon who rules blood and a human.

They say that when a vampire drinks someone's blood, they absorb that person's soul and use it to amplify their own powers.

They say that a vampire can transform a part of their body—or even the entirety of it, along with their clothes—into winged beasts to fly about at will.

They say that vampires possess powers that far exceed those of most races and that their physical strength rivals even that of giants.

They say that by employing sorcery, a vampire can take the form of mist, wolves, or even their ancestral dragons.

They say that vampires halt their growth when they are at peak physical condition and have lost the very concept of aging.

They say there are differences between individual specimens and that some vampires stopped growing while retaining the appearance of a child.

They say it takes years to turn another race into a vampire and that the process requires the act of sharing their blood.

They say that vampires do not rely on either Elementals or the magic of the natural world and can convert blood into magic power.

They say it is only an old wives' tale that vampires are weak to sunlight

DEAD MOUNT DEATH PLAY

Episode ❽: Barrier of Coursing Blood

by Ryohgo Narita

Manga exclusive bonus short story

What had attacked Shagrua was a being known as an enemy of the world.

A notorious assassin famous the world over.

She went by the name Crimson Snow.

A vampire who drained the blood of her targets.

She did not, however, drink the blood she took. Instead, she saturated the earth around her in crimson as she went on her way, using it as her limbs and, when necessary, her weapon.

Drinking the blood would have temporarily boosted her abilities, which is what vampires used blood for.

But she didn't think favorably of such things, choosing instead to put the blood to work as her minions.

As if she were letting something from those she'd killed act on her behalf.

■ ■ ■

Vampires.

In the world where the Kingdom of Nyanild and Byandy Empire existed, they were but a race that blended seamlessly into society.

The vampires of that world shared some aspects in common with the legends told on Earth, and they also had qualities that were vastly different. Most notably, society there acknowledged the existence of such beings.

Even so, that isn't to say that there were hordes of vampires, and as far as population went, vampires made up a rather small minority. However, due